Eye View

Eye View

By

Gloria Casey

CAMBRIDGE
SCHOLARS
PUBLISHING

Eye View, by Gloria Casey

This book first published 2009

Cambridge Scholars Publishing

12 Back Chapman Street, Newcastle upon Tyne, NE6 2XX, UK

British Library Cataloguing in Publication Data
A catalogue record for this book is available from the British Library

ISBN (10): 1-4438-1389-3, ISBN (13): 978-1-4438-1389-1

This book is dedicated to my wonderful husband Val for all his love and encouragement in all of my artistic endeavours.

Also to my parents Michael and Rita Phayer, who gave me my first camera that started me on the artistic road.

TABLE OF CONTENTS

ACKNOWLEDGEMENTS

I would like to thank Dr. Micheal O'hAodha and Peter Morgan for their contributions to this publication.

INTRODUCTION

THE PRESENCE OF THE ABSENCE

PETER MORGAN
ARTIST/LECTURER – LIMERICK SCHOOL OF ART & DESIGN

Photography has become the most disseminated medium in the world, with its relatively short history it has captured everything!

In many respects there is nothing left to photograph and yet we continue to make photographs, so the question remains why do we make photographs?

On looking at Gloria's photographs I am reminded that it is the everyday, the ordinary that we have lost sight of. We fail to see what is essentially in front of our eyes. When Gloria takes a stroll there are two seagulls watching and waiting, the observer being observed.

Likewise there is a presence of the absence. I am looking at Gloria's photograph of two deckchairs; they are empty, billowing in the breeze that is present but not seen. The occupants have departed and the deckchairs are awaiting, even inviting us to sit down and gaze off into that distant space, the soft blue with the sound of the waves gently crashing, the endless repetition both inviting and comforting.

I am looking at one of her photographs sitting in my room; it's 10:30 at night, outside the stars are shining brightly, the fire has warm embers glowing in the hearth and I am looking at a photograph of a bright red delivery truck, it's parked but there is something I have not told you..!

Which is like the photograph of the teddybed that is both very sad and very funny at the same time. So these photographs need to be seen and they need to be read, they invite us to speculate, to ponder the "what's not said." We are involved in a narrative that is elliptical, simple and quite complex, both challenging and reassuring, both contradiction and fact. And all this is happening at the same time, which is confusing as the waves come crashing down only to repeat what we thought we had glimpsed as the snow settled around our feet.

After the snow and before the seagull has landed there is a moment of anticipation, willing the obvious into fact. We know what is about to happen and the camera with all its sophisticated technology freezes a moment. Cartier Bresson spoke and acted in that moment. When he coined the phrase "the decisive moment" he was poised and waiting to capture the aesthetics from the flux of life, that is not stationary but constantly in motion. Others have questioned this decisive moment and have made photographs in what is now the "indecisive moment" revealing a more casual, less formal aesthetic.

Once the boundaries have been broken, the possibilities of seeing and recording expand and a new reality is presented which soon becomes the orthodoxy. But just as we start to accept this new reality along comes Geoff Dyer and he proposes "the ongoing moment" which points to another way of understanding. That is essentially the brief history of photography, which repeats certain themes through sucessive generations of picture makers.

Gloria observes and records the rain drops on glass, and as viewers we are reminded of the minute detail of something we see and yet fail to see. This is a moment, a fragmentary moment taken out of time, place or space, but none the less poignant. I am left wanting, trying to fill in the blanks, attempting to read between the lines to answer the questions that are not really questions but are an invitation to look at what I already know but have forgotten to see. Which is like "the photograph waiting to be taken just outside your door; all you have to do is open that door".

ESSAY – HISTORICAL & CONTEMPORARY ANALYSIS OF THE MANIPULATED IMAGE

GLORIA CASEY

For thousands of years humans have had a desire to have representations of their surroundings and events in a pictorial form. This can be evidenced by the early cave paintings of animals and people found in France and South Africa. These artists had no reference points and were not bound by any rules or conventions; they drew what was important to them in their daily lives. According to Dr. Nigel Spivey who noted in a BBC TV program, *"The caves are thought to be religious sanctuaries the act of drawing an animal had some ritual significance"*[1]. As far back as 787AD The Council of Nicea recognized the importance of images when it decreed *"representations of divine figures and stories served as 'books for the unlettered' as reminders of the divine qualities of Christ and the Saints, and as vehicles for devotion"*[2].

Over the centuries artists have utilised various techniques and devices, as they were developed to aid them in the construction of their images. Aristotle noted in the 4th century BC that a narrow beam of bright light entering a dark room projected an image of the scene outside. During the Renaissance, this idea was taken a step further when Leonardo da Vinci described in his Notebooks "*...images of illuminated objects penetrate into a very dark chamber by some small round hole...you will receive these images on a white paper placed within this dark room...you will see all the objects on the paper...upside-down"*[3]. This became known as the Camera Obscura (Italian for dark room) and was used by artists to help them to accurately depict perspective in their images.

---

[1] *How Art Made The World* was broadcast on BBC Two on Monday's at 2100 BST. http://news.bbc.co.uk/2/hi/science/nature/4532785.stm
[2] Kemp, M. [Ed] *Oxford History of Western Art* pg 155
[3] Richter, I. [Ed] *The Notebooks of Leonardo da Vinci* pg 115

Perhaps the development of photography was inevitable. A way had to be created to capture a likeness in a more efficient manner other than painting and drawing, as this was both time consuming and expensive. John Berger states that, *"Images were first made to conjure up the appearance of something that was absent...An image became a record of how X had seen Y"*[4]. Is it possible that this is what drove the early pioneers to push the boundaries with regard to producing images?

Various people were involved in moving forward the limitations of conventional image making. At the beginning of the 19th century, the race began in earnest to produce the world's first photograph. Most activity took place between 1826 and 1839 and involved such noted people as Joseph Nicephore Niepce, Louis-Jacques-Mande Daguerre and William Henry Fox Talbot.

One person whom I find particularly intriguing is Hippolyte Bayard who is believed to have created the first staged photograph.

Fig 1:

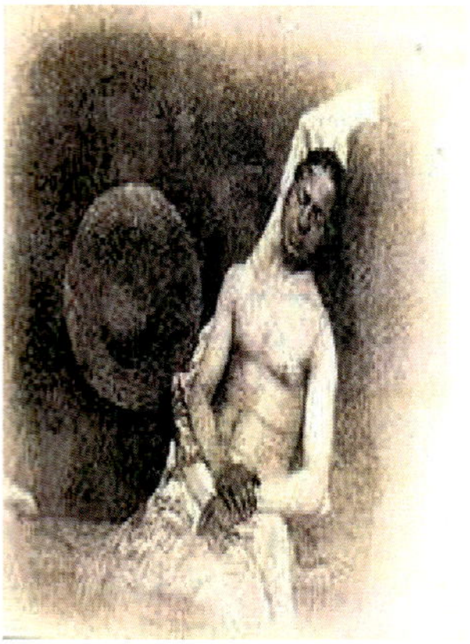

***Drowning Man* 1840** by Hippolyte Bayard
"The corpse which you see here is that of M. Bayard, inventor of the process that has just been shown to you. As far as I know this indefatigable experimenter has been occupied for about three years with his discovery. The Government which has been only too generous to Monsieur Daguerre has said it can do nothing for Monsieur Bayard, and the poor wretch has drowned himself. Oh the vagaries of human life....! ... He has been at the morgue for several days, and no-one has recognized or claimed him. Ladies and gentlemen, you'd better pass along for fear of offending your sense of smell, for as you can observe, the face and hands of the gentleman are beginning to decay"[5].

---

[4] Berger, J. *Ways of Seeing* pg 10
[5] http://www.rleggat.com/photohistory/history/bayard.htm

In *Drowning Man* he depicted himself as a dead man, who has drowned himself because the French Government at the time gave all the credit to Daguerre for producing the first photograph, while he was given none even though he had contested that he had been the first to produce a photograph with his method. He didn't in fact drown himself but he did stage the image as a protest to the French Government. As can be seen from the illustration, he obviously had a sense of humour for he was inviting people to look at the photograph and then informs them, *"you'd better pass along for fear of offending your sense of smell, for as you can observe, the face and hands of the gentleman are beginning to decay"*[6].

By day Bayard was a Civil Servant, but in his spare time he dabbled in photography and claimed that a friend of Daguerre had asked him to postpone his announcement, thereby allowing Daguerre to take all the glory that was bestowed by the French Government. Many of Bayard's works are now in the Getty Museum and he was the first photographer to be granted a *mission héliographique* by the Commission des Monuments Historiques to document architecture in France[7].

Not everyone at the time greeted the development of photography as something positive, Charles Baudelaire, a French poet and art critic in 1859 is quoted as saying *"If photography is allowed to supplement art in some of its functions, it will soon have supplanted or corrupted it altogether"*[8].

Photography didn't take over from conventional art practice but it did signify a change in the style of work that artists produced. With the invention of the camera, artists who used the medium of paint were no longer confined to depicting realistic images as the camera could now produce these more efficiently.

The development of the camera proved to be a double-edged sword. While it was accepted that a photograph could be a portrayal of an event as it occurred, it created an argument as to whether the resulting image could be considered as art. This argument was settled in 1861-62 when a judge in Paris stated *"photographs could be...products of thought and spirit, of*

---

[6] ibid.

[7] http://www.getty.edu/art/collections/bio/a1876-1.html

[8] op. cit. Kemp, M. [Ed] *Oxford History of Western Art* Pg 674

taste and intelligence, bearing the imprint of a personality and thus works of art"[9].

The development of The Box Brownie in 1900 by George Eastman revolutionised the whole process of photography. It was portable and one roll of film took a hundred images. The camera was then posted to the factory where the film was processed, reloaded and returned to the user. The introduction of this camera to the market finally brought the medium of photography to the masses. No longer was it the prerogative of the elite to have images of them, for one US dollar anyone could have a photograph of themselves or anything else they liked. As a result for the first time the whole image making process was democratised[10].

From its inception, photography has struggled against various prejudices from whether the image is a true representation of a given moment to whether the image can be considered as art, as mentioned previously. This discussion is particularly relevant today due to the popularity of digital technology and its potential to manipulate everything about the image so that it no longer resembles what was originally seen. Some contemporary commentators have a problem with this as has been noted by Martin Lister when he states that some commentators have, *"issued warnings of the 'you can no longer trust your eyes' variety*[11]*"*.

But can we ever say about any image, whether it is a painting or a photograph, that it was a true representation of a given moment? Does it really matter, particularly if the image is going to be used for artistic purposes and not for example in a newspaper – where it might be relied on for its authenticity? Is it possible that the photographer as artist could be seen as continuing in a long tradition of manipulating images? Susan Sontag states, *"People want the idealized image: a photograph of themselves looking their best"*[12]. This is a comment that has permeated throughout the history of representation, but the '*idealized image*' is not necessarily reality.

When we talk about images that are used for art purposes, could it be suggested that we have always manipulated the scene to reflect what the

---

[9] Honore, H. *A World History of Art* pg 694
[10] http://www.kodak.com/US/en/corp/features/brownieCam/index.shtml
[11] Lister, M. *the photographic image in digital culture* pg 1
[12] Sontag, S. *On Photography* pg 85

artist wanted to say, no matter what medium was used? While it's true to say the camera can only take what is in front of it, this doesn't allow for the hand of the photographer as artist.

A painter can organize his surroundings prior to beginning a painting so that he has his reference points to work from. If the work is being painted outdoors, the painter can "borrow" a tree from here, a rock from there, if it suits the composition better. While a photographer cannot "borrow" a tree etc. to improve the composition, the image can be manipulated later through the use of various computer packages to include items that were not in the scene, if that is how they choose to work.

This is not a new phenomenon. Oscar Rejlander in 1858 produced an image called *The Two Ways of Life*.

Fig. 2:

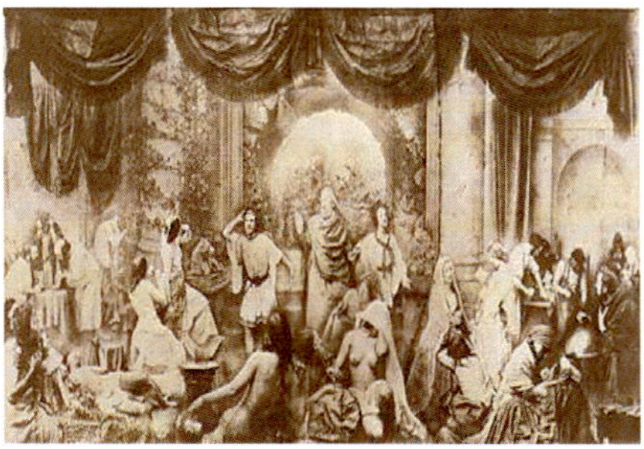

He chose the medium of photography to tell the story of two young men who are trying to decide between the good and the evil way of life while being guided by an older figure. Considering photography was in its infancy this image is an amazing feat.

It was impossible for Rejlander to capture this as one image at that time; he had to take a photograph of each figure individually. There are at least twenty-five figures in various poses that required each of the models to stay perfectly still for a number of minutes, in order to capture them correctly. Obviously, as Robert Leggat suggests, the event as we see it, never took place[13]. Rejlander is believed to have used at least 30 different negatives to produce the image[14].

A criticism often levelled at photography is that because it is produced by a mechanical medium, it doesn't possess the artist's hand.

[13] http://www.rleggat.com/photohistory/history/rejlande.htm

[14] Weaver, M. Essay *O.G. Rejlander, The Two Ways of Life* in *A New History of Photography* [Ed.] By M. Frizot pg 188

Fig. 3:

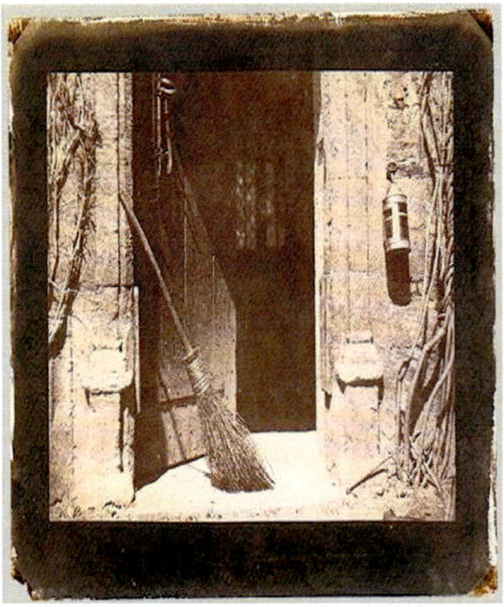

In a photograph by Fox Talbot called *Open Door* it could be argued that it clearly shows the hand of the artist. It could be suggested that he manipulated his surroundings by creating a staged reality, with the broom in bright light, propped against the slightly open door, showing the darkness inside, he's making the viewer curious as to what's inside. It could be said he was viewing the scene as a painter would by creating light and shade but using a camera rather than a brush and paint.

If we compare *Open Door* with contemporary work *Orange twine on black corrugated, spattered with lime* by internationally recognized artist/lecturer, Peter Morgan.

Fig. 4:

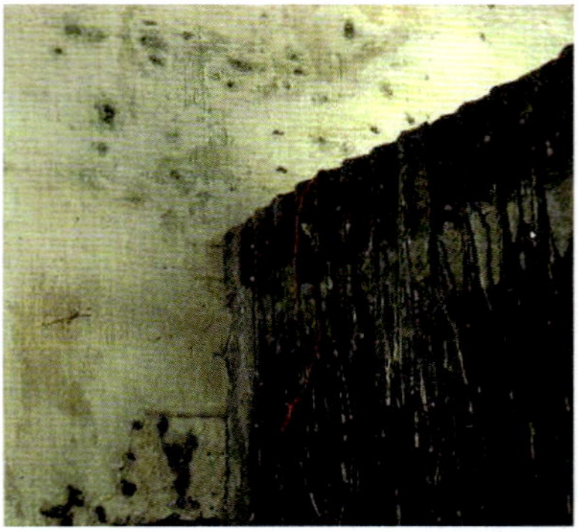

At first glance, one could almost mistake this image for a painting. The image is reminiscent of Talbot's *Open Door*, as previously mentioned. It appears to the viewer that this is a true and natural representation of the scene as it was captured. There are no obvious indications of any prior intervention or manipulation by the artist. In reality its casual appearance masks the true level of effort that has been expended in *'making'* this image.

In an interview with the author, Morgan stated, *"This image was made, very slowly with a tripod and a medium format camera. It's very carefully set up, taking many hours to get the lighting and composition correct"*[15]. The image depicts a corrugated iron fence that had been dribbled with what appears to be black paint, with orange twine draped over it. One can see the grey of the iron where it hasn't been painted in black. The white wall behind the fence has been spattered with a green like substance that looks as though it's eating into the wall and giving it a corroded look. The image has a very textural quality to it, as if one could reach out and touch it. Morgan explains that this image was, *"the wall of a shed, with a lime washed wall at the back that is decaying with time. It's a divide between two sheds with black corrugated iron that used to have a piece of wood that was running across the middle part here which is now missing hence you get the black dribble of the bitumen"*[16].

Upon further discussion, Morgan related how he had carefully manipulated the scene by placing the orange twine in a specific location. It did not just happen to be there, it was placed in that position by the artist. He further enhanced the scene using extra lighting. Yet he has managed to retain a natural quality to the image. As Morgan stated his purpose was not to make it look obvious that the image had been specially lit or manipulated through the use of a computer package. He was aiming to achieve a painterly quality to the image, so that it would look natural to the viewer[17].

His intention was to, *"try to bring something to the attention of others, to look at something we might otherwise overlook and not see. I like the simplicity of it, but I'm trying to lift something beyond what it actually is"*[18].

---

[15] Casey, G. Thesis *Historical and Contemporary Analysis of the Manipulated Image, in Particular Relation to its Deployment in Photography* Appendix
[16] ibid. Appendix
[17] ibid. Appendix
[18] ibid. Appendix

Fig. 5:

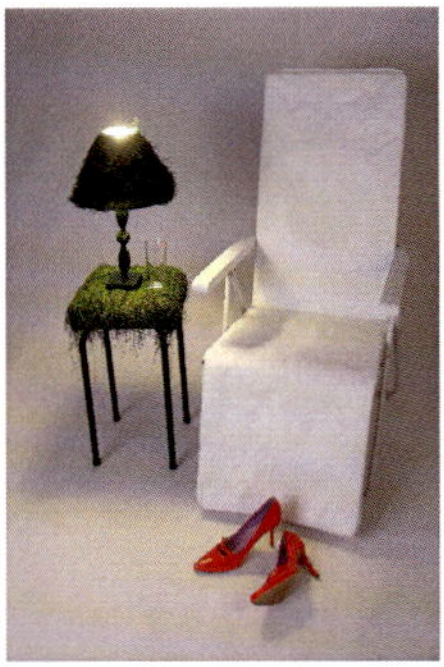

On a photo shoot for *Quiet Moment*, by the author, in the midst of placing the particular objects, the realization dawned that what was taking place was not just the taking of a photograph for documentary purposes, but also the creation of an artwork in its own right. The process transcended the mere capture of a moment in time to a piece of work that could be considered art in itself as distinct from the objects being photographed. As in Talbot's and Morgan's photographs, the interplay of light and shadow, through the use of atmospheric lighting, helped to create a more natural appearance.

The juxtaposition of the objects, the interchange of colours from the green of the grass to the painted red shoes against the stark white background, was carefully staged prior to the photograph being taken. The objective of this representation was to take everyday objects and transform them in a number of ways, including utilizing organic and traditional artistic mediums.

What this tableaux is endeavouring to encapsulate is the essence of someone who might have used these item's. We can see the imprint of the body on the chair, the light is left on, the lipstick on the glass – the viewer is left to imagine who the person might be, without having to see them.

In conclusion, photography due to its *"the camera can't lie"* [19] tag, occupies a strange position in society that continues to generate debate. Certainly, the camera as a mechanical device can only record what is in front of it. However, the person controlling the camera has many options open to them for image manipulation and now with the sophistication of digital technology there are no limits to what can be achieved if so desired.

Some artists such as Peter Morgan and the author prefer to use more traditional methods such as either deliberately staging the scene through the use of colour or lighting etc., or by utilising what is available in our environment. While other artists, prefer to employ all that new technology has to offer them in the form of computer editing software.

[19] Druckery T. *Digital Dialogues – Photography in the Age of Cyberspace* pg 18

Photography since its invention in the 1800's has generated much discussion as to the truthfulness of the image. While the camera as a mechanical instrument cannot lie, the representation of truth is in the hands of the photographer and their choice as to whether to use the various techniques available to them, such as the use of different lens, exposure times, lighting, cropping, airbrushing, computing etc.

With the advent of digital technology, commentators such as Ritchin have stated that it signals *"the end to photography as we have known it"*.[20] This echoes Charles Baudelaire's statement in 1859, *"If photography is allowed to supplement art in some of its functions, it will soon have supplanted or corrupted it altogether"*[21]

While the former statement has a certain validity, in so far as it could be suggested that this is the end of analogue photography, as we have known it. Just as in the 1800's with the introduction of photography it was considered to be the end of painting as it had been practised up to that time. In reality this did not happen, but then as now, with each development come new opportunities as a direct result of the technical innovations that have taken place. Rather than supplanting or corrupting traditional art, photography facilitated a whole new medium for the creation of new art forms.

The advent of the digital camera and PC based editing software has not led to the death of photography; in fact, it is more alive than it ever has been. Statistics published by BBC News January 2002 show that in October 2001, *"more than 21 million US computer users turn to digital photography"* and *"use of photo-editing software in the home is up 27%"*[22]. In this case, one might suggest, the statistics speak for themselves.

---

[20] Kember, Sarah, *Virtual Anxiety – Photography, new technologies and subjectivity* pg 18

[21] op. cit. Honour, H. *et al A World History of Art* pg 674

[22] http://news.bbc.co.uk/1/hi/sci/tech/1779800.stm

INTERVIEW WITH GLORIA CASEY

DR. MICHEAL O'HAODHA

Can you tell us a little bit about your background Gloria – you were born in Limerick?

I was born and educated in Limerick City and attended the Limerick School of Art and Design as a mature student. I gained my Degree in fine art specialising in Sculpture and Combined Media in 2006.

How did you become interested in photography Gloria?

I have been interested in photography for a very long time. When I was younger, I enjoyed taking photographs of family and friends, it's always been important for me to have a record of events as they were happening. I still remember my first serious camera – an Olympus Trip that my father bought for me on a trip. I had many years enjoyment from this camera.

Do you work in any other art forms? – Can you tell us a bit about this?

Yes, I like to use different media to create my work. If I have an idea for a piece of work, I give it a lot of thought as to the most appropriate media to use which best expresses my thoughts. In the past I have created installation pieces using found objects. I like to experiment with mixed media, taking ordinary, everyday objects and transforming them utilising organic and traditional mediums. My objective is to transform the mundane and ordinary into what I hope are thought provoking pieces that encapsulate elements of mystery and humour. This in turn feeds in to my photographs.

Can you give us some information about some of your previous projects and what you are working on at the moment?

In 2005, I was selected from over a 1,000 submissions, to take part in the Iontas Small Works Art Competition and was honoured to be awarded second prize overall for the works *Teddybed I and II*. This was an annual (now a bi-annual) competition for contemporary artists living in Ireland and held in the town of Sligo by Sligo Art Gallery.

The Adjudicator Dr Teresa Millet, IVMA, Valencia said of the work *"Teddy Bear I and II shows a traditional folding summer lounger for the terrace or garden, on which a small teddy bear is quietly resting. As a worthy follower of Duchamp in the 21st century, with the selection of objects that attain the status of a work of art as a result of the way in which they are seen and manipulated, Gloria demonstrated impeccable execution and great sense of humour which made me decide to award her the second prize in the competition."*

I created this work to exist on two separate levels, firstly, as a photograph of the installation that exists as a record of the work and as a piece of art in its own right. Secondly, as an installation where the item itself could be seen and interacted with. For the installation piece, I attached a voice box under the bed and when it was touched it activated sensors that caused the mouth of the bear to move, talk and laugh.

In 2007 I had another work selected for the Iontas Small Works Art Competition. This work was titled *Gone but not Forgotten.* This photograph depicts a chair with an open red book placed on it and a tray with a mug covered in grass nearby.

This work was part of a series that I had been working on that were inspired as a result of attending a number of funerals for friends and acquaintances the previous year. I was also influenced by Roland Barthes book, Camera Lucida where he describes how following the death of his mother he searched for a photograph, which for him would describe her essence[1]. What I wanted to reference in this work was the spirit of the people who may have used these objects. I wanted to create a questioning approach to the work i.e. Where is the person using these items? Will they come back? Are we intruding on a quiet moment?

This theme was further developed in the photographs *Hoover*, and *Lamp & Stool* which I exhibited in Dublin and Enniskillen. Some of the objects have been covered in grass to represent our life cycle. We come into this world as a seed, we grow and then eventually we decay. But we remain in the memory of others. This is exemplified by the use of a transient organic medium, which is juxtaposed with the photographic image frozen in temporal space.

Many of the items were rescued from being thrown out. They were deliberately chosen to give them a new sense of purpose. I reclaimed the

---

[1] Barthes R. *Camera Lucida* pg 66

manmade and allowed nature to eventually take over by letting the work decay gracefully in the open air. This again reinforces the temporary nature of human existence "*The grass withereth and the flowers fadeth*[2]"

How do you like to take your photographs? What is your preferred way of working?
My method of working depends on what I want to say with the work. When I've been working on an installation piece, I have taken some of the objects into a studio, out of their context and photographed them against a white background. This allowed me to focus on the object and eliminate the 'noise' that sometimes intrudes into an image.

To a certain extent this approach continues with the landscape/seascape photographs where I like to zoom into what I'm photographing to try to capture the essence of the scene and allow it to create it's own narrative such as can be seen in *Evening Stroll.* I captured these two birds while they were strolling along the beach in Bournemouth, United Kingdom. I could just imagine their conversation 'whose turn is it to catch dinner'.

What other photography and (other art form) projects are you working on now?
At the moment I am influenced by what I see in nature. In particular the sea and in the action of waves, how they build up and curl into a tunnel before crashing down into a crescendo of white foam, each one different from the last. I like to keep an open mind to the beauty of the environment that surrounds us. I could be walking through a park and capture squirrels dashing playfully about or walking the beach and catch birds foraging in the seaweed for food.

I am also interested in using some of the images to influence my painting. Currently, I am working on a series of paintings where I'm focusing on the actions of people i.e. walking, surfing, sitting etc. Just like in some of my photographs, they are painted against a white background, allowing the viewer to fill in the negative space with their own imagination.

---

[2] *The Bible* Isaiah chapter 40 verse 8 (Isaiah 40:8)

Some artists feel the need to travel beyond their own country in search of artistic inspiration- are you one of these?

I have travelled extensively over the years in Europe, the Middle East, the Caribbean and North America and I never travel without a camera. Travel has influenced my work to a degree and it certainly broadens the mind. In terms of artistic inspiration, I don't feel it is necessary to travel to gain inspiration. I am a firm believer that a photograph is waiting to be taken just outside your door; all you have to do is open it.

Bibliography

Name	Title	Publisher	City	Year
Barthes, R.	*Camera Lucida*	Vintage	London	1993
Berger, J.	*Ways of Seeing*	Penguin	London	1972
Druckery, T.	*Digital Dialogues – Photography in the Age of Cyberspace Vol. 2 No. 2 Autumn*	Ten 8	Birmingham	1991
Frizot, M. [Ed]	*A New History of Photography* Weaver, Mike Essay *O.G. Rejlander, The Two Ways of Life*	Konemann	Koln	1998
Honore, H. *et al*	*A World History of Art*	Laurence King	London	2002
Kember, S.	*Virtual Anxiety* Photography, new technologies & subjectivity	Manchester University	Manchester	1998
Kemp, M. [Ed]	*The Oxford History of Western Art*	Oxford University	Oxford	2002
Lister, M. [Ed]	*the photographic image in digital culture*	Routledge	London	1995
Morgan,P. *et al*	*Revealing Angelica*	Road Books	Cork	2005
Sontag, S.	*On Photography*	Picador	New York	1977

Websites

http://www.rleggat.com/photohistory/history/bayard.htm
http://www.rleggat.com/photohistory/history/rejlande.htm
http://www.getty.edu/art/collections/bio/a1876-1.html
http://www.kodak.com/US/en/corp/features/brownieCam/index.shtml
http://news.bbc.co.uk/1/hi/sci/tech/1779800.stm
http://news.bbc.co.uk/2/hi/science/nature/4532785.stm

Illustrations List

Against The Odds

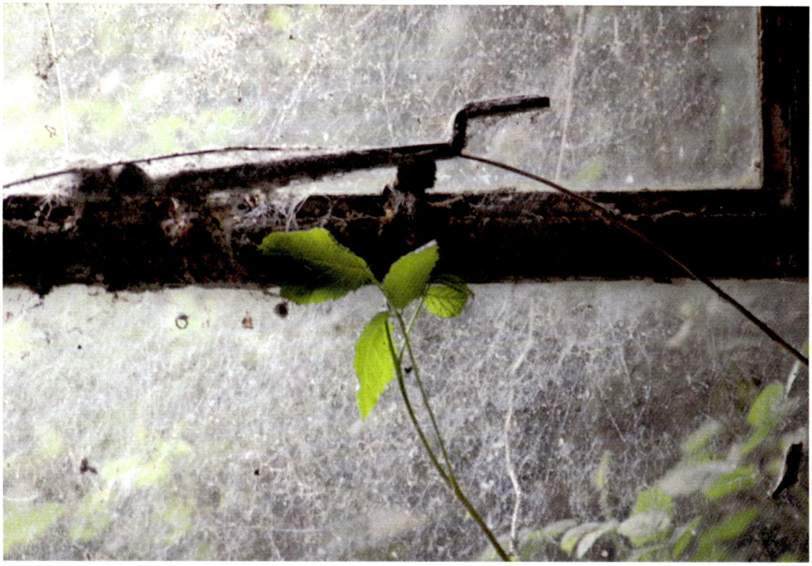

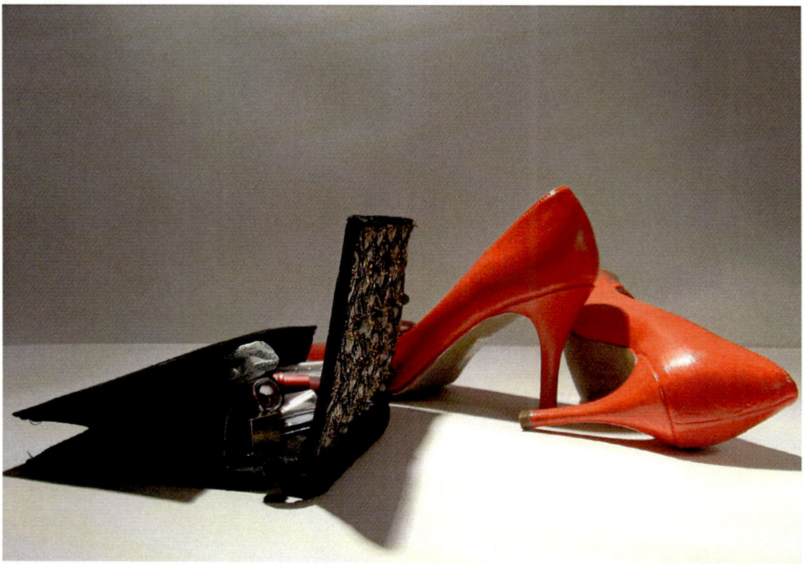

Almost Ready

Alternate Reality

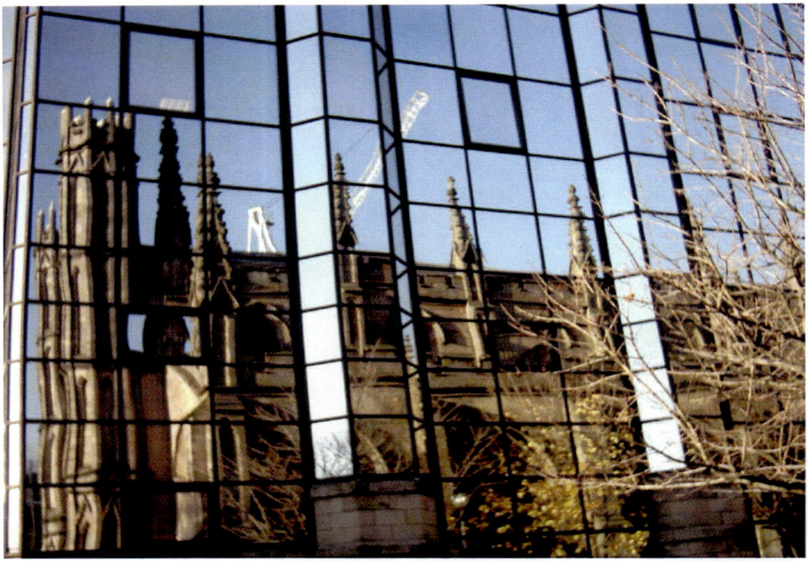

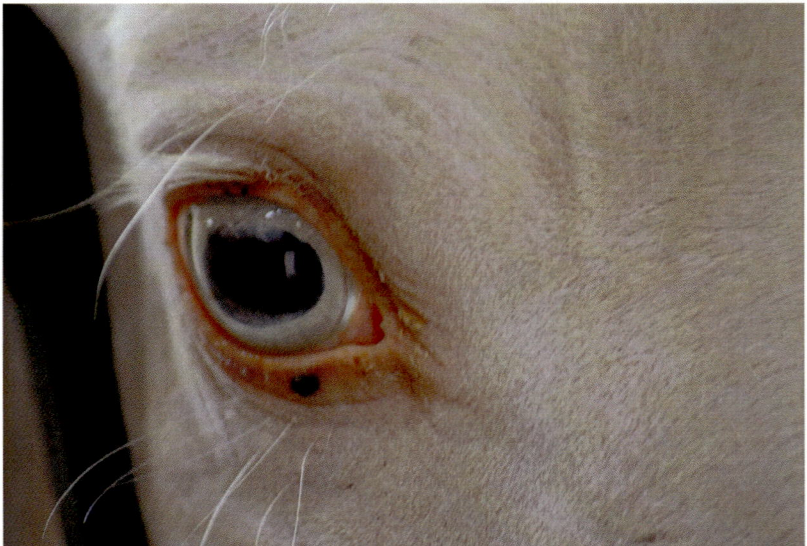

Bailey

Bridge Over Flowing River

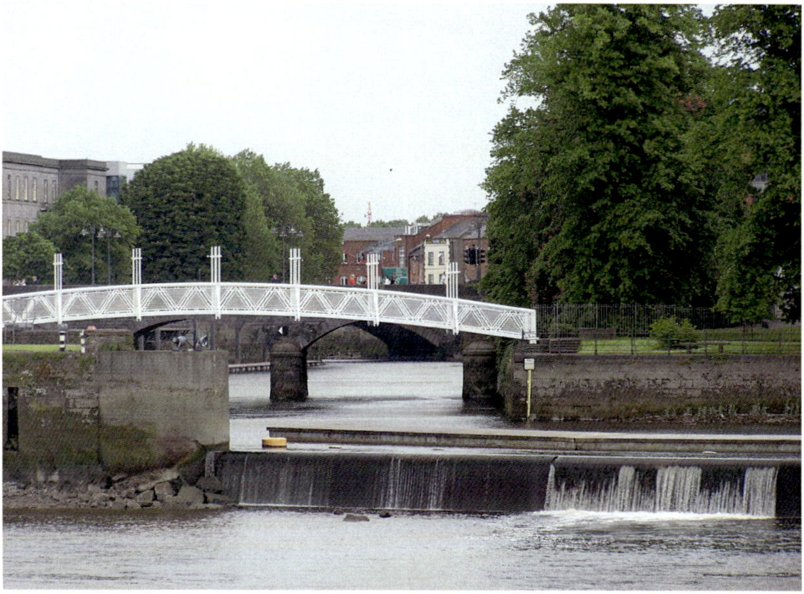

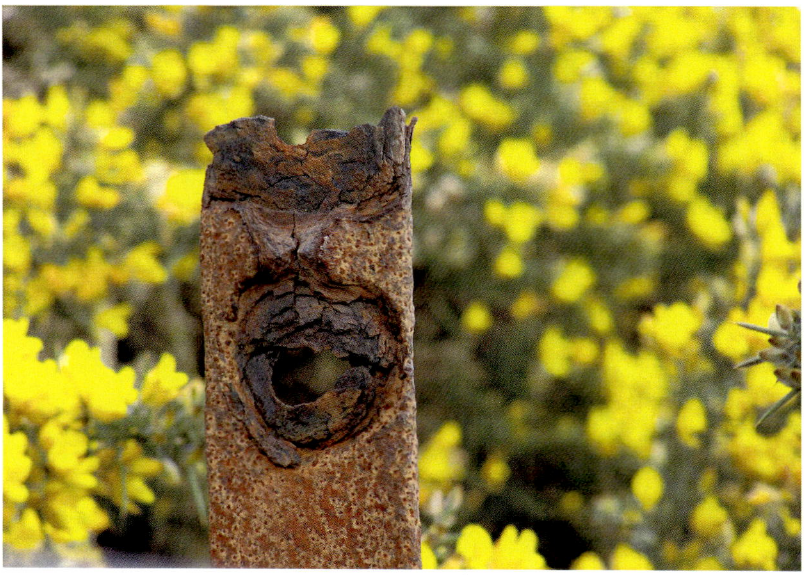

Browned Off

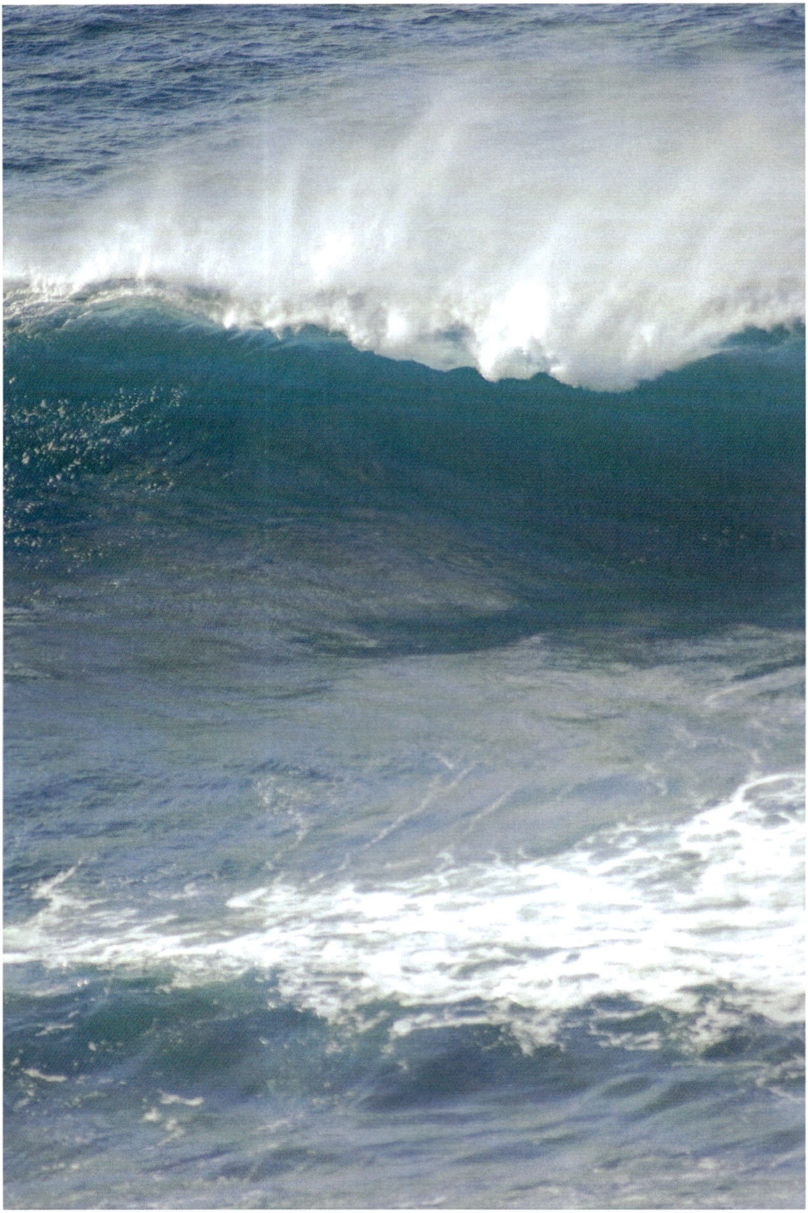

Catching The Wave

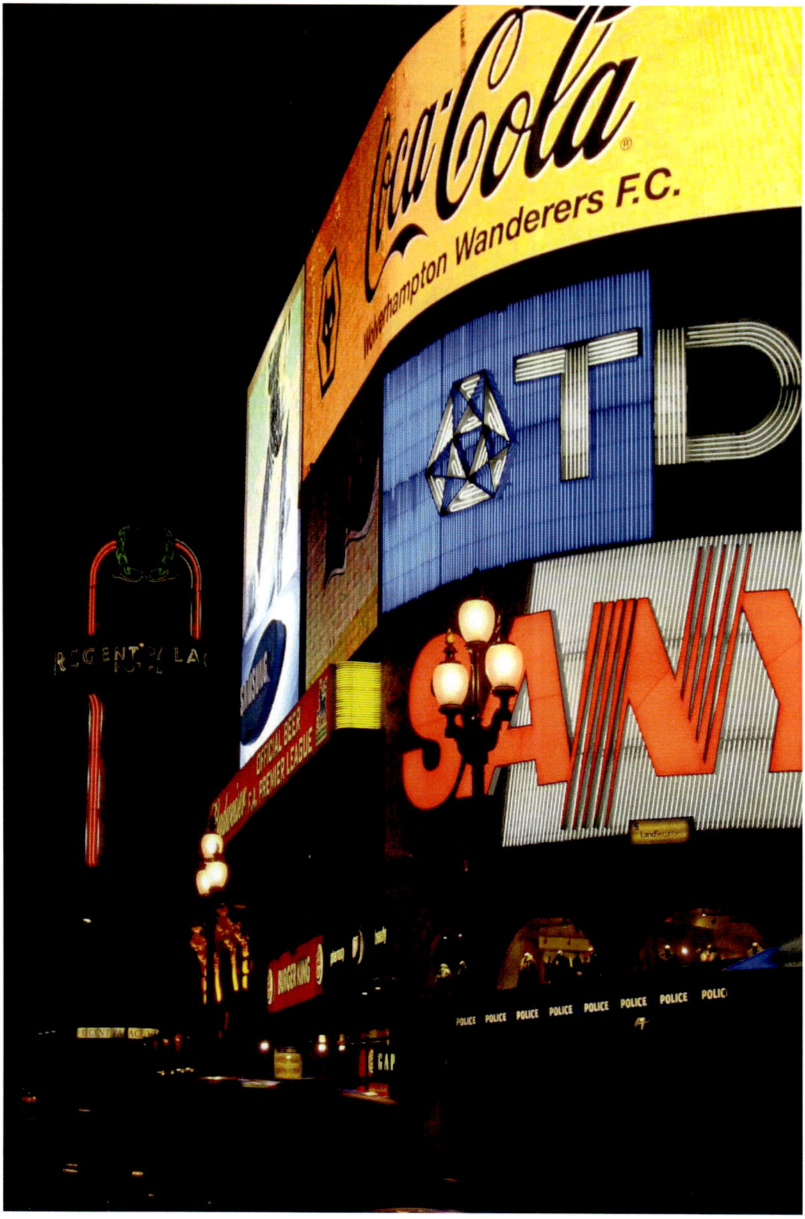

Circus Lights

Comes Fully Fitted

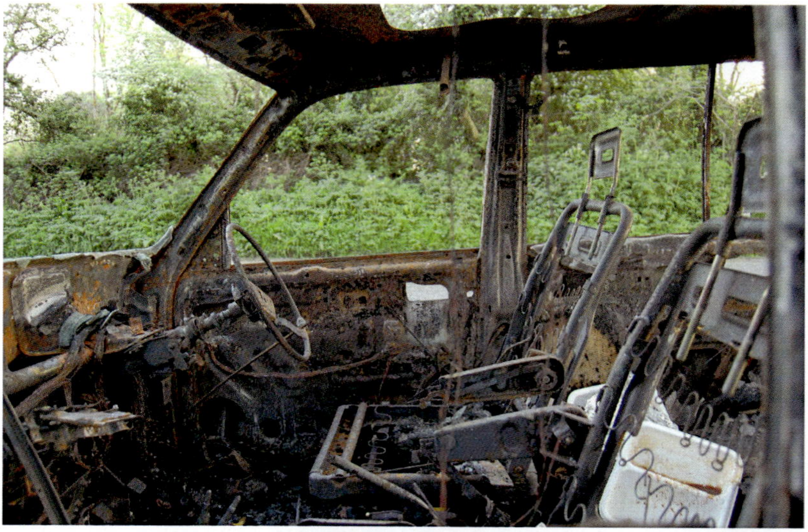

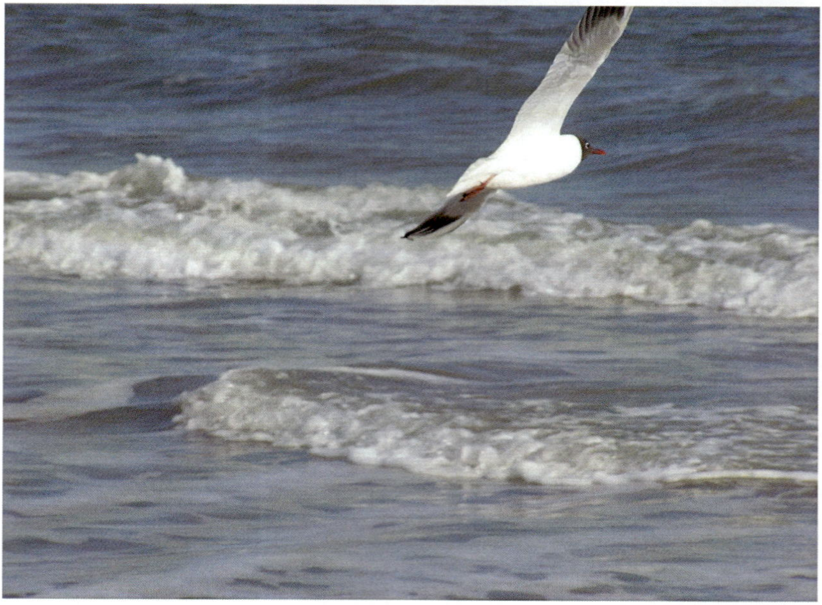

Coming In To Land

Daisy

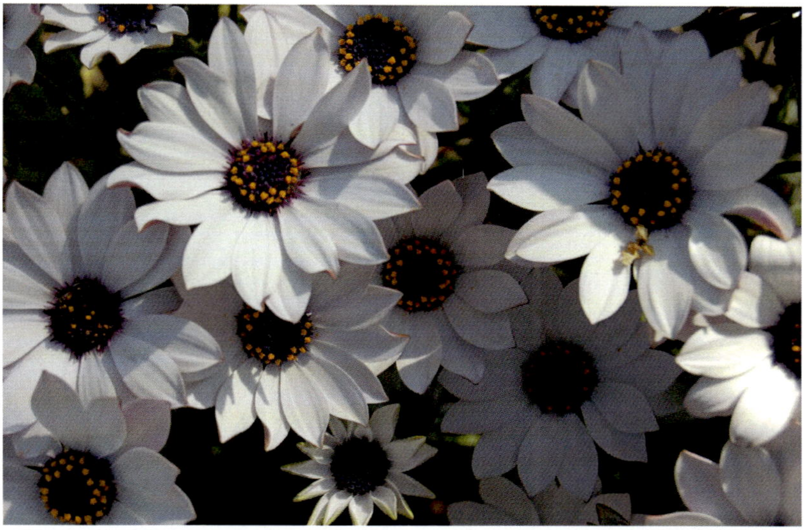

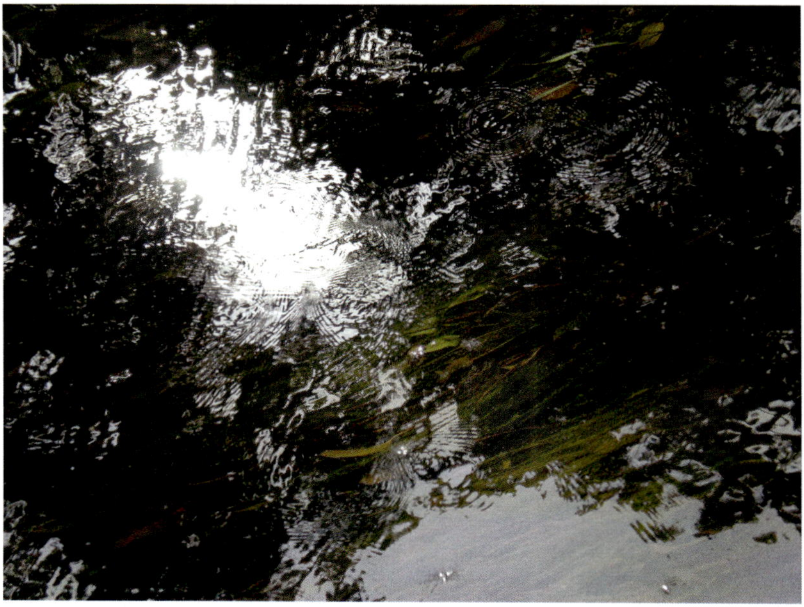

Dappled Light

Decay

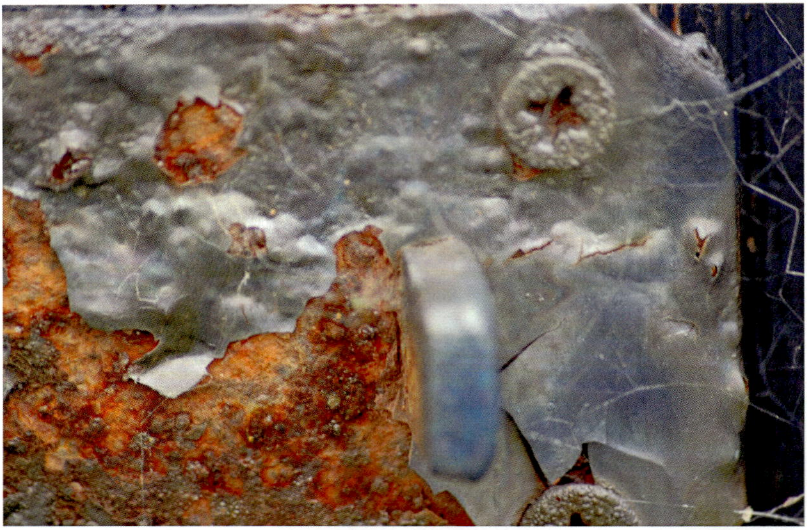

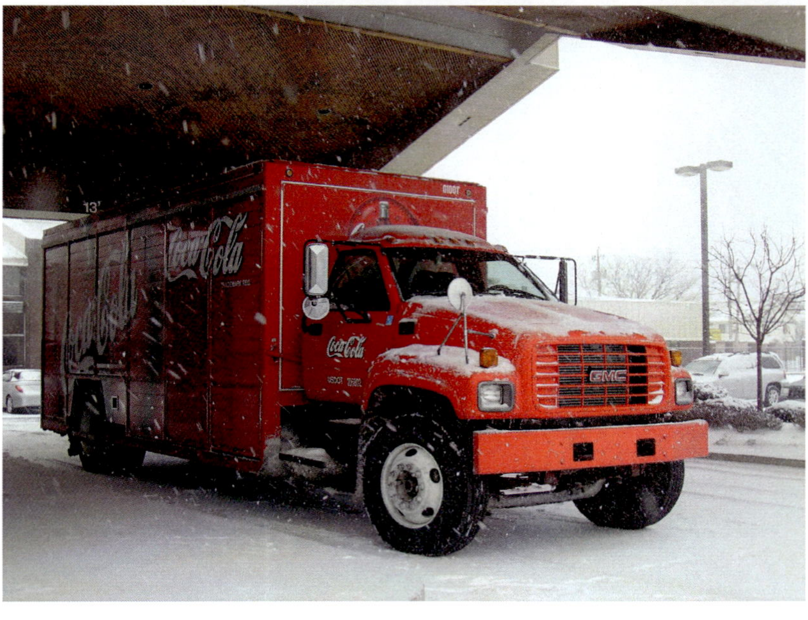

Delivery

Don't Miss The Bus

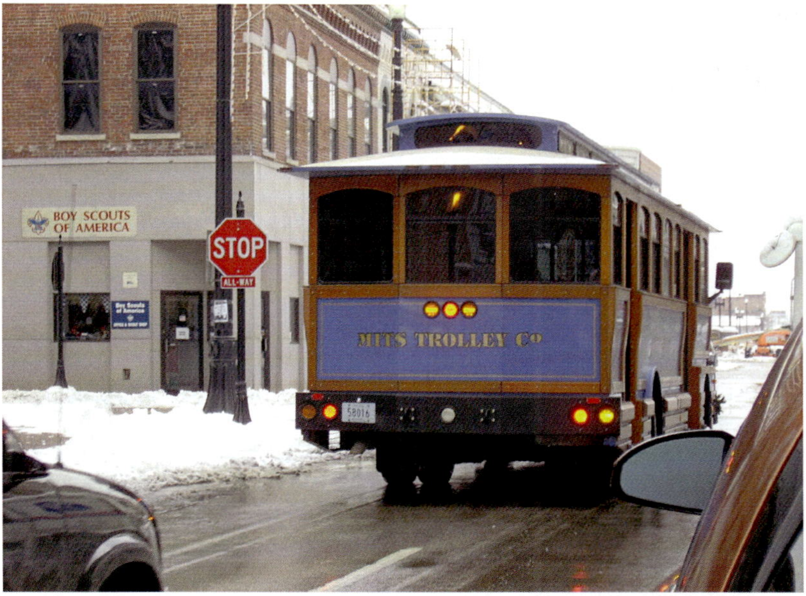

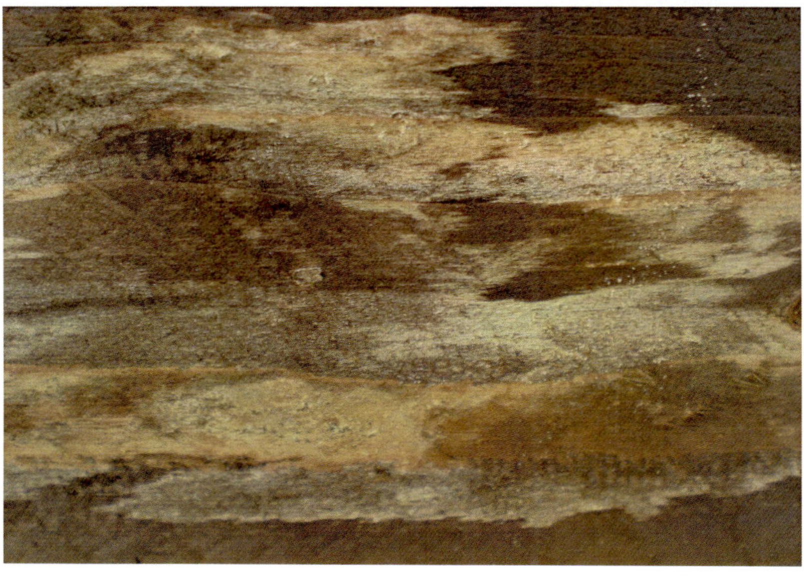

Drift Away

Drip, Drip

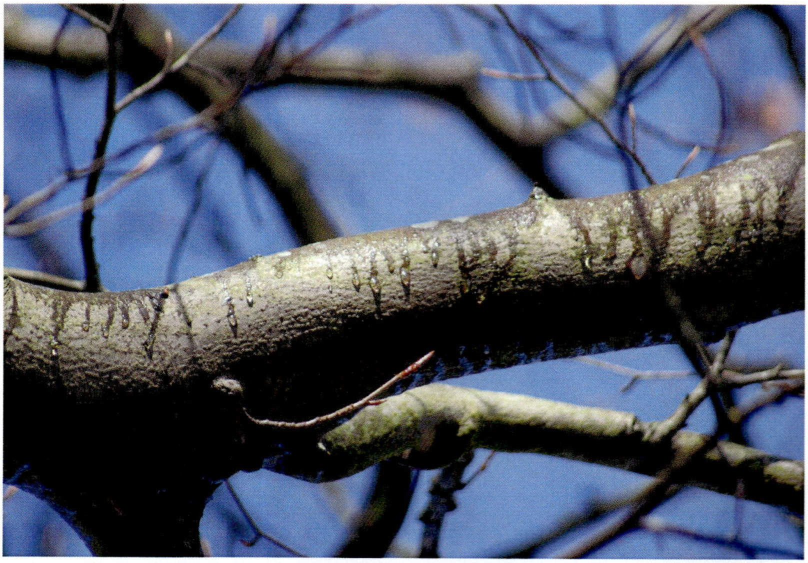

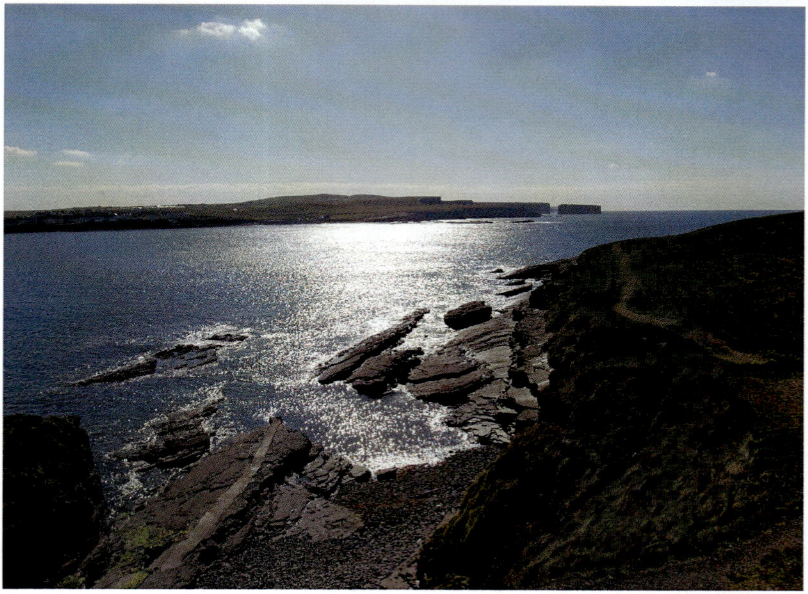

Evening Light

Floating

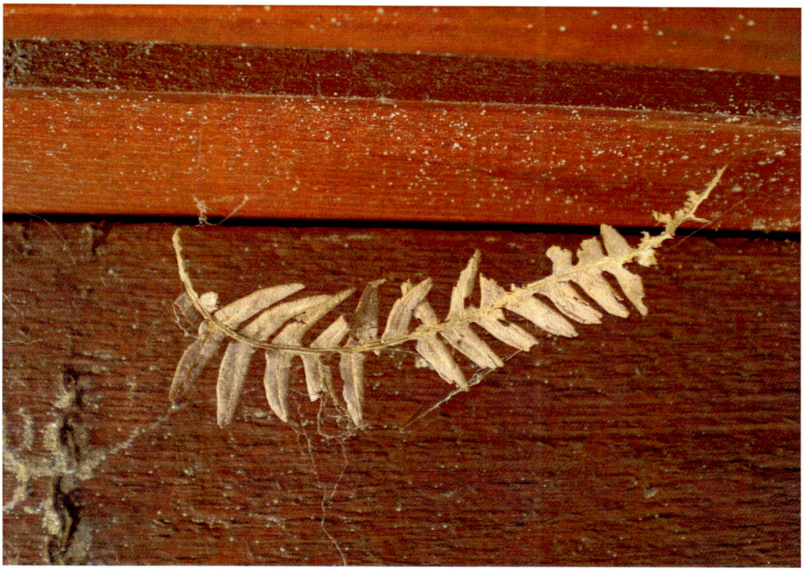

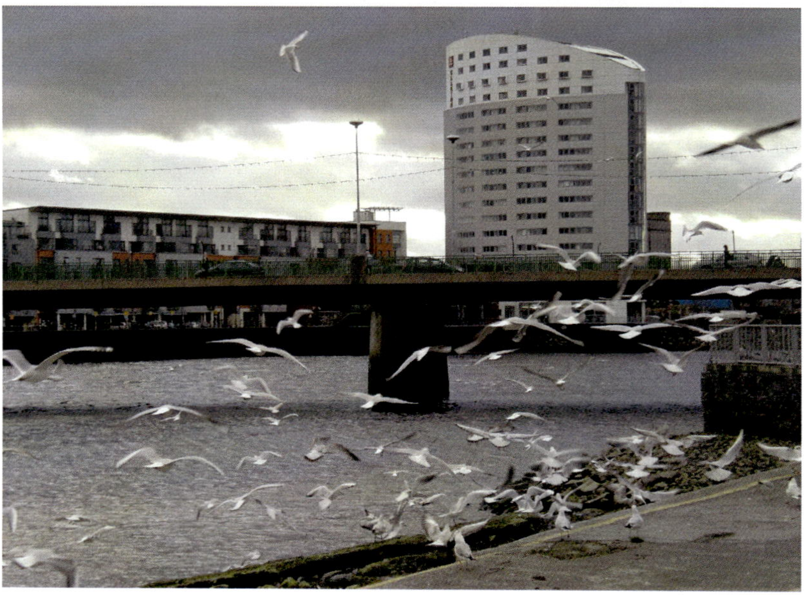

Foods Up

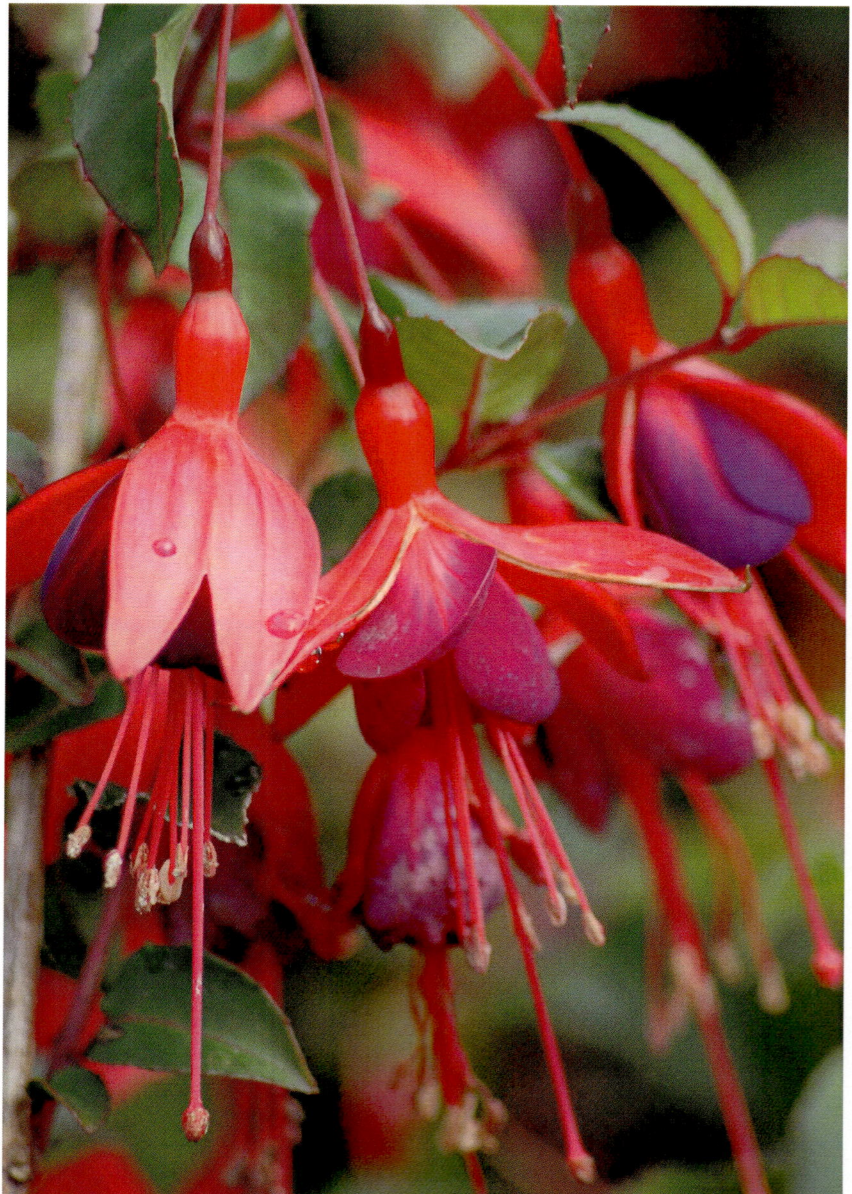

Fuchsia

Gone But Not Forgotten

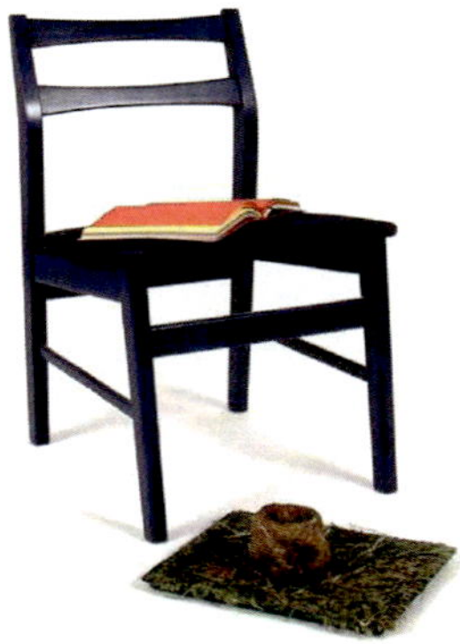

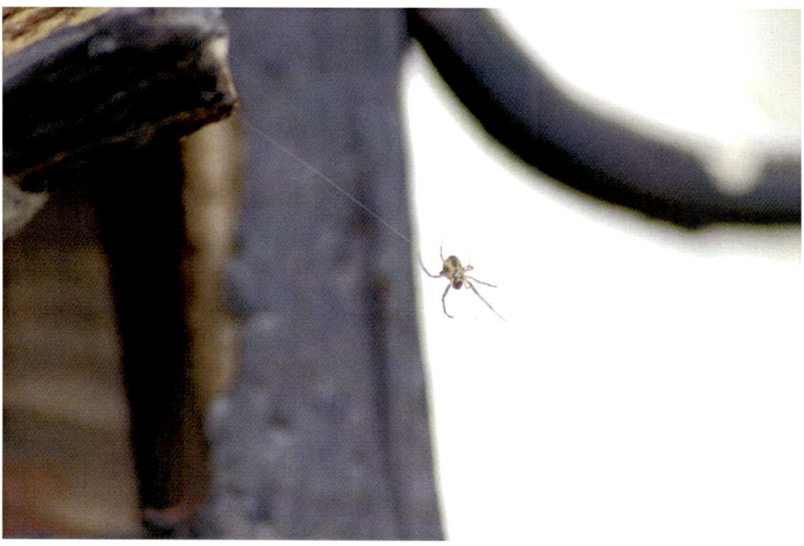

Hanging By A Thread

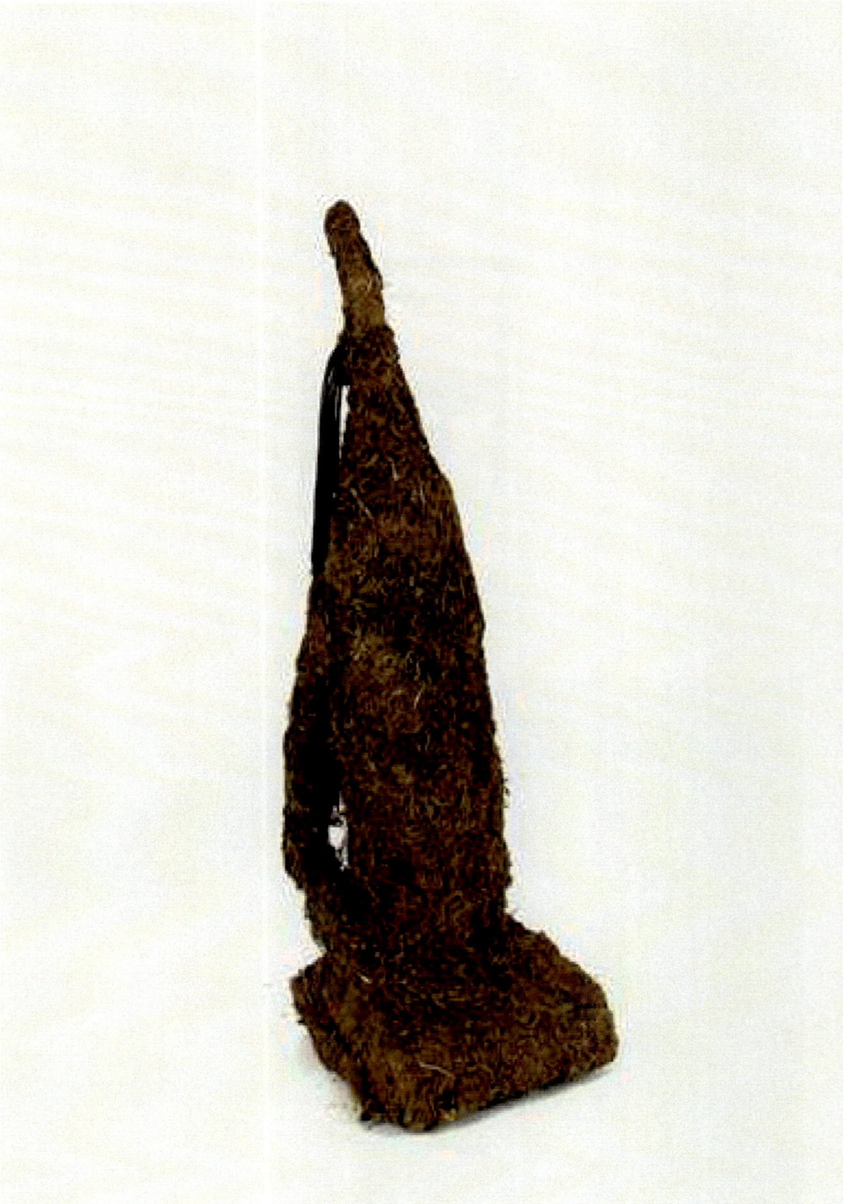

Hoover

I Won't Fall…Honestly

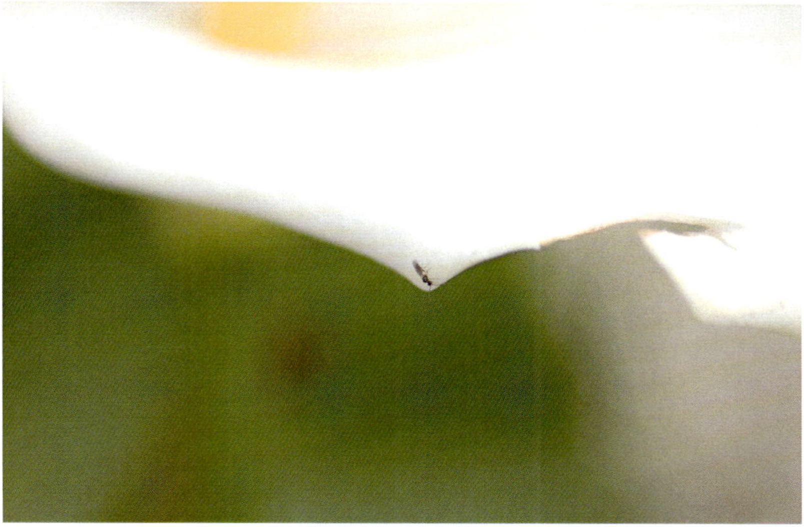

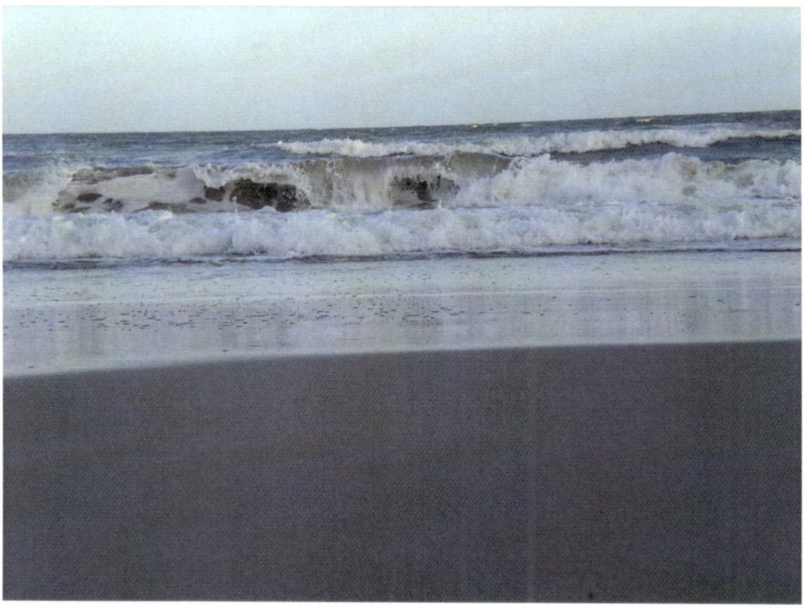

Incoming

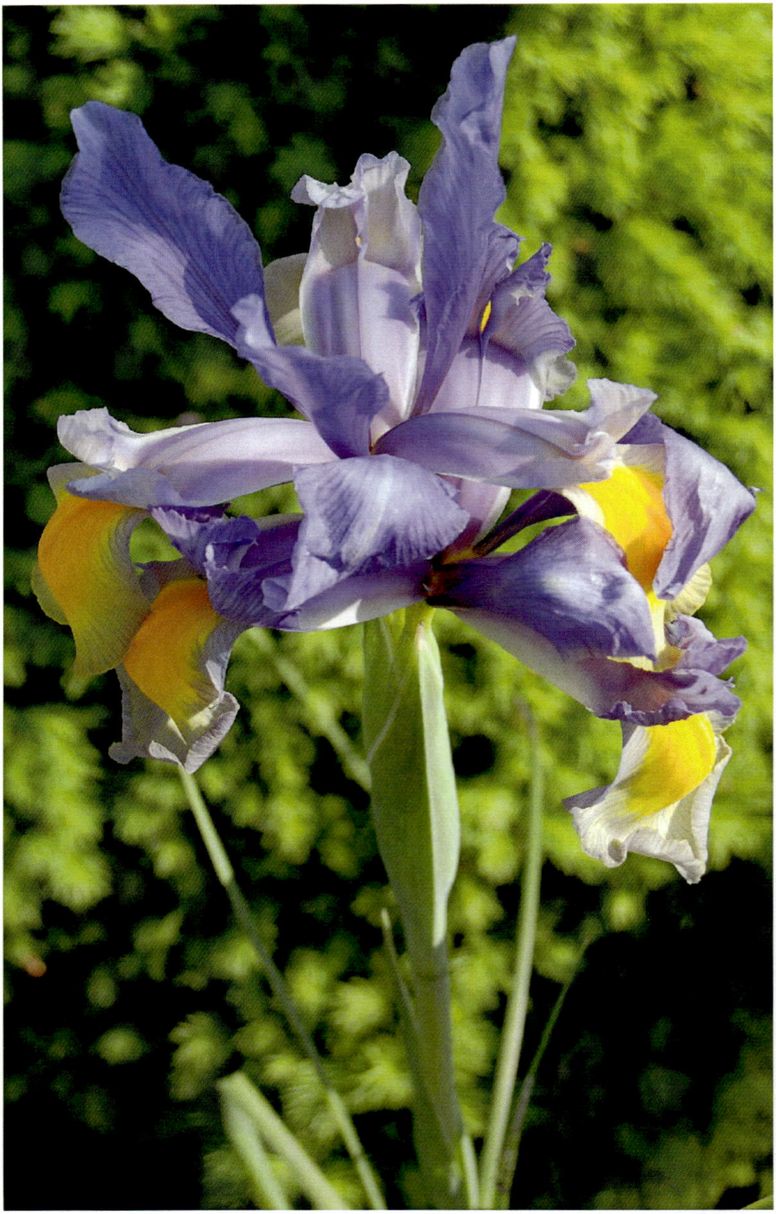

Iris

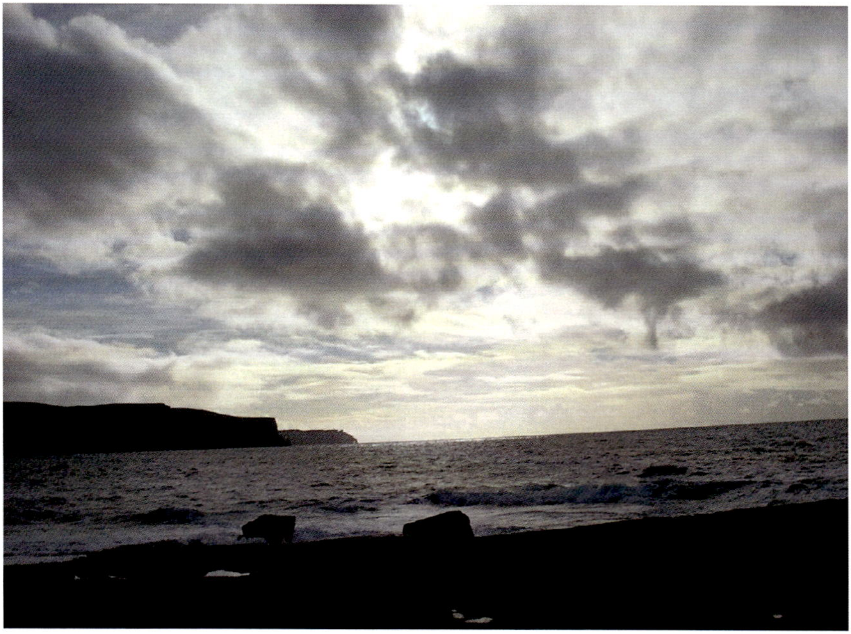

It Might Rain

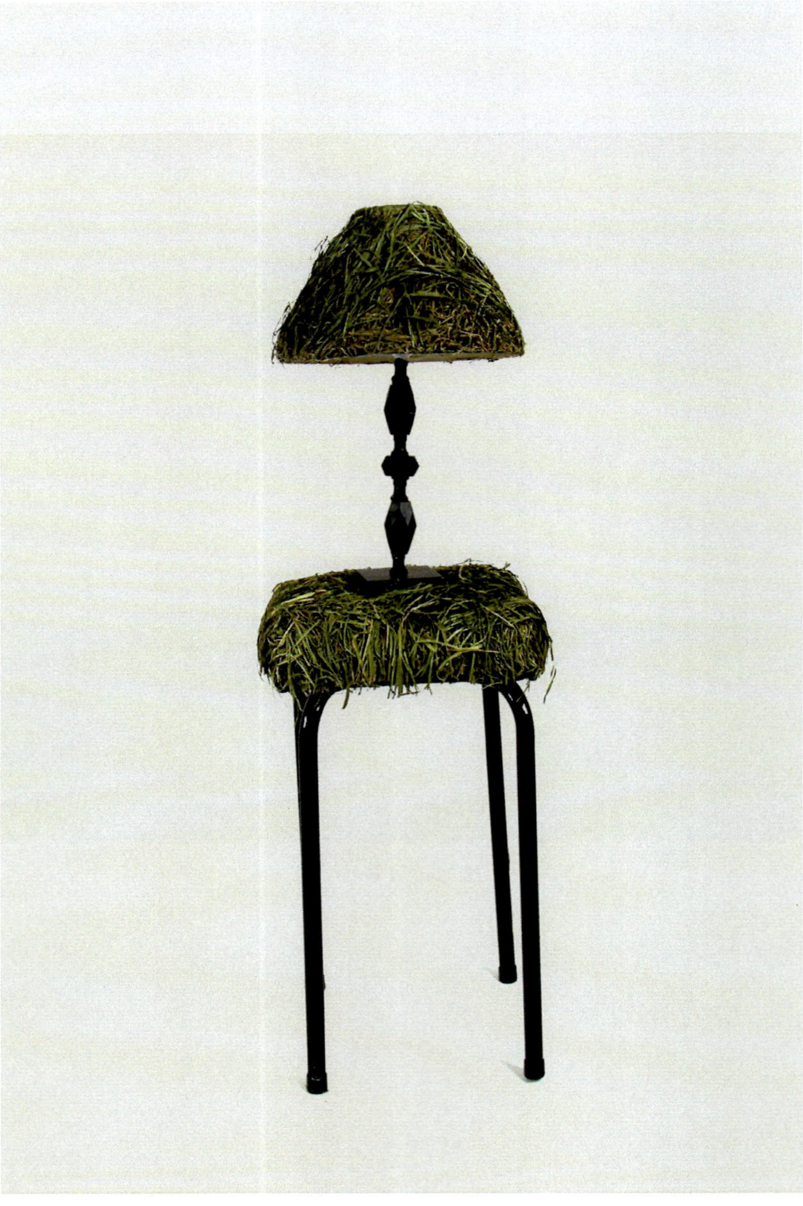

Lamp & Stool

Lichen Covered Wall

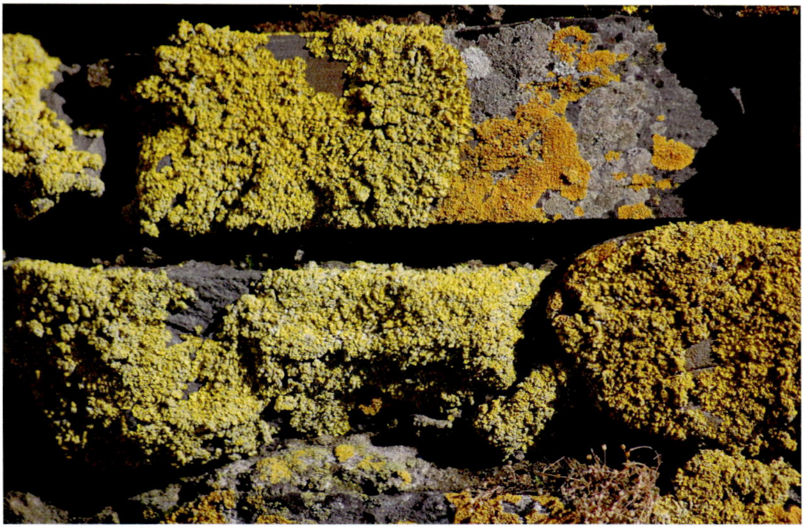

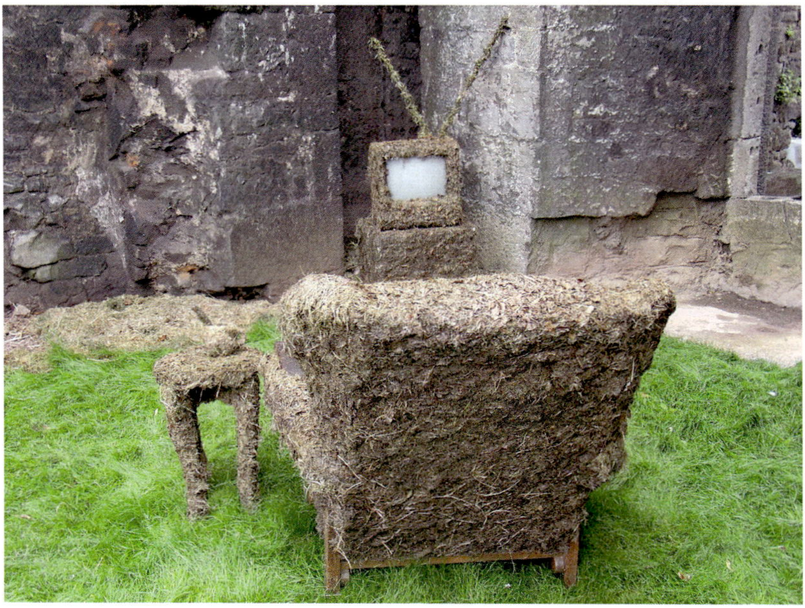

Life in The Castle

Long View

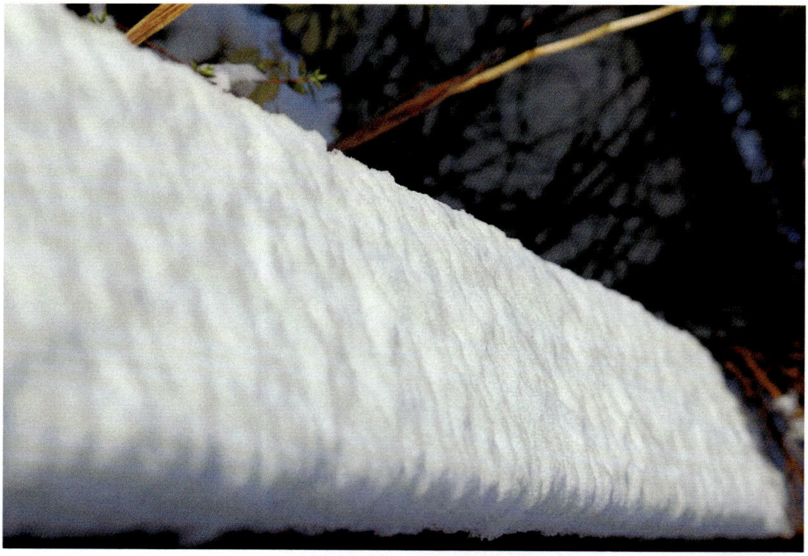

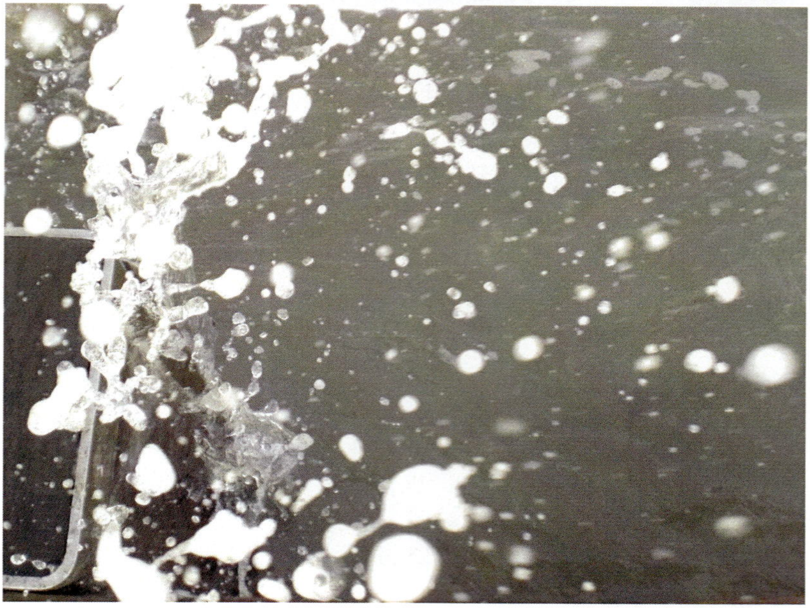

Mind Where You Stand

Mystery

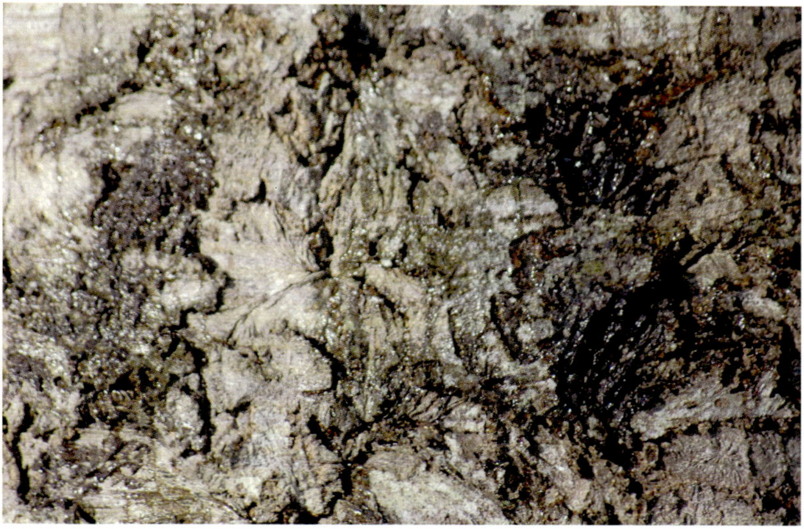

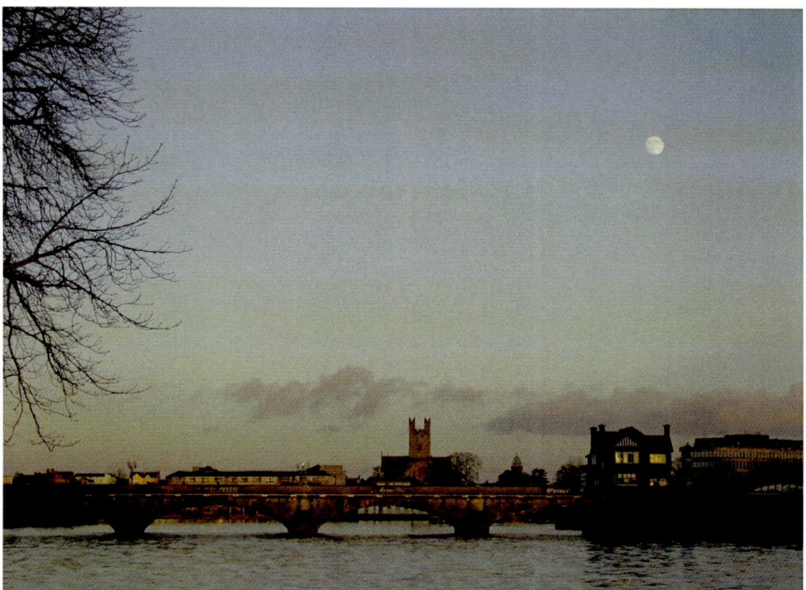

Nearly Dark

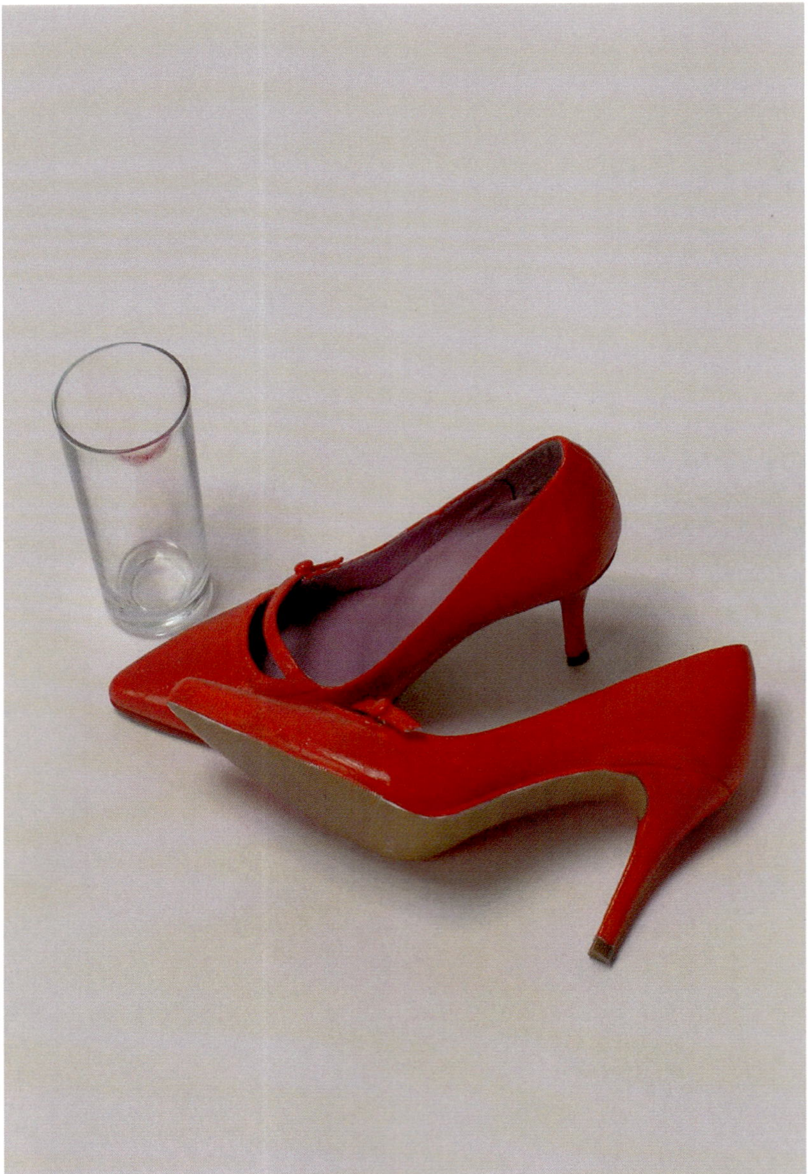

Night Out

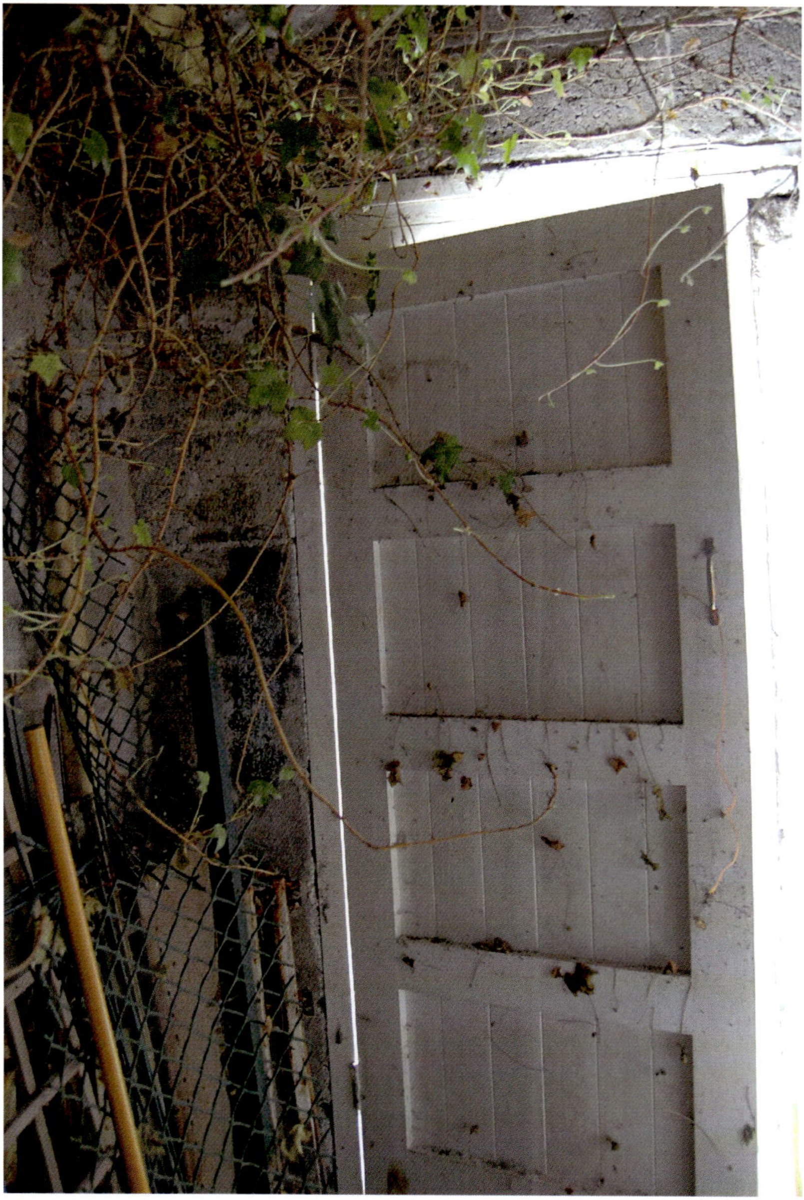

Open Door

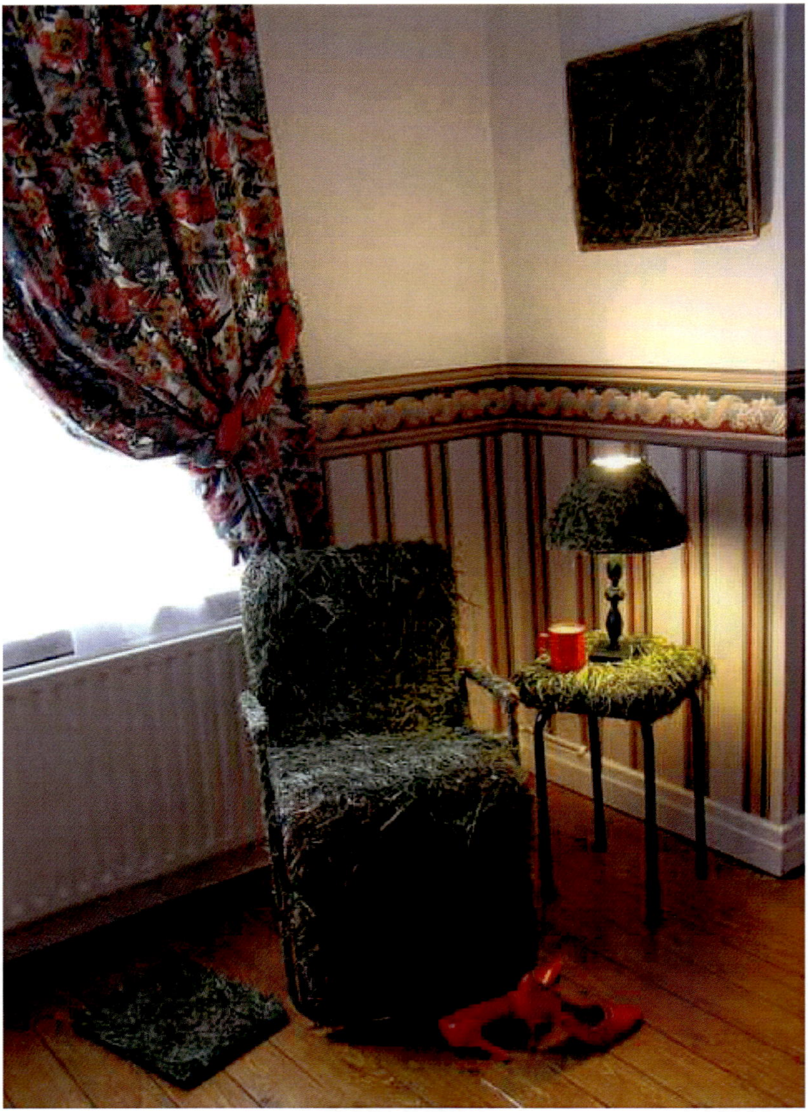

Outside In

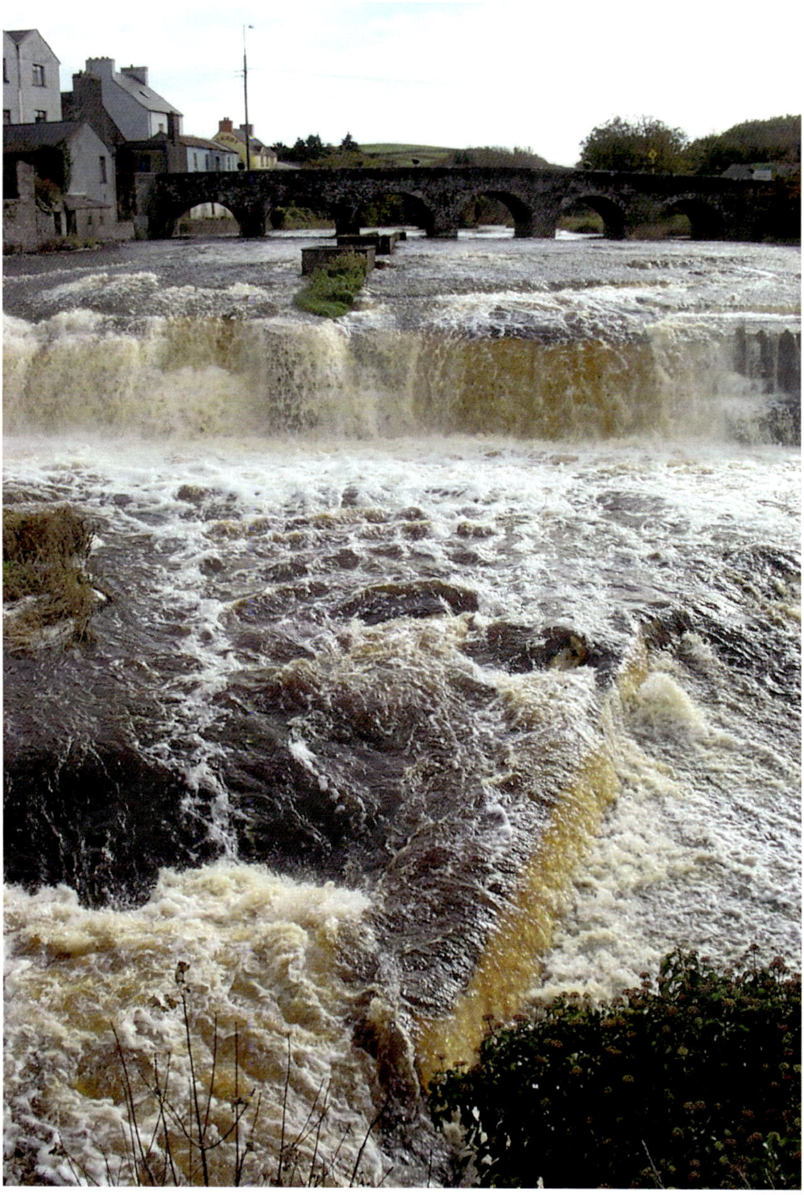

Overflowing

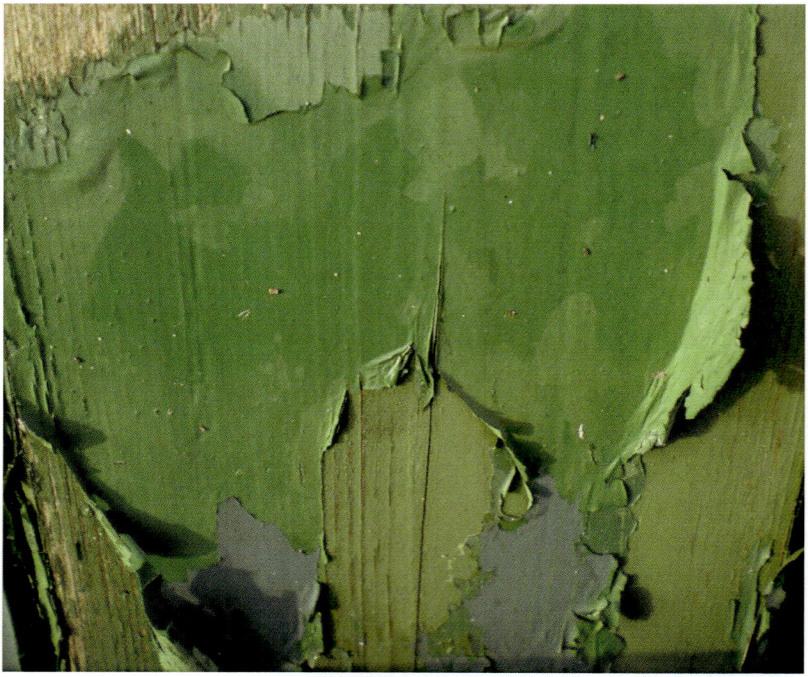

Peeling Gracefully

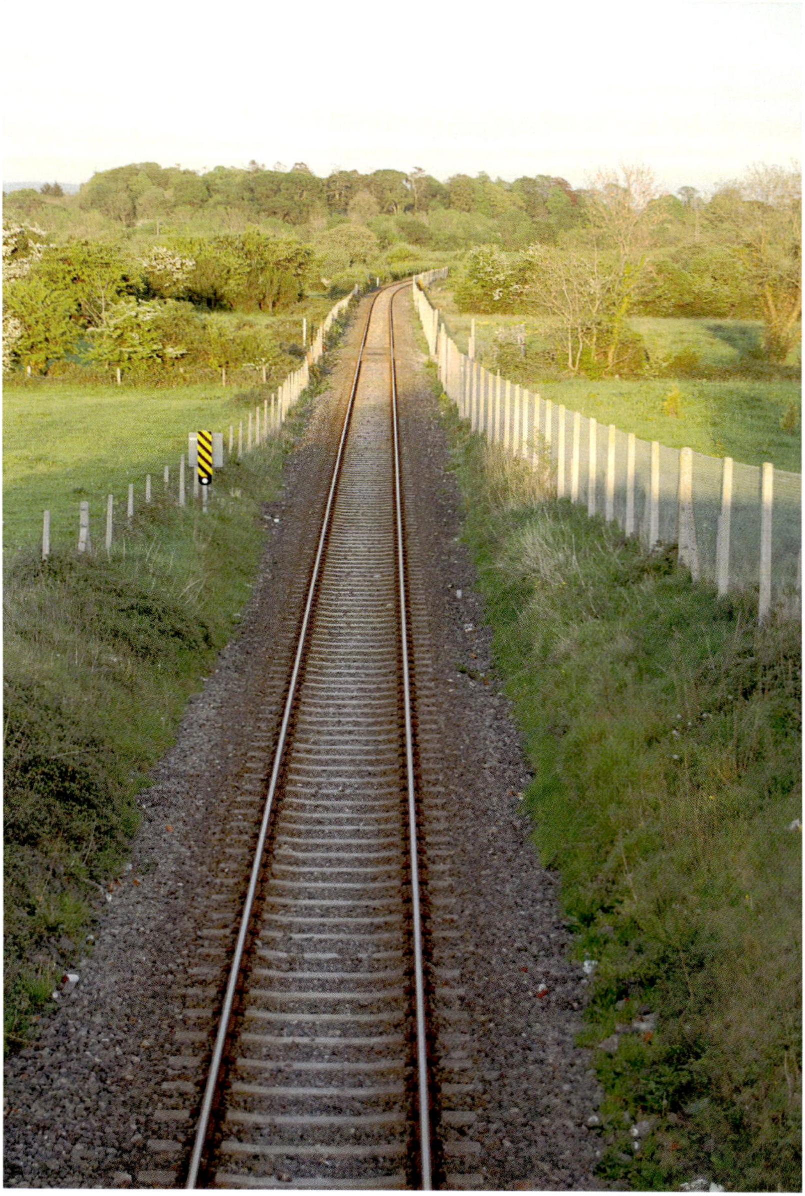

Perspective

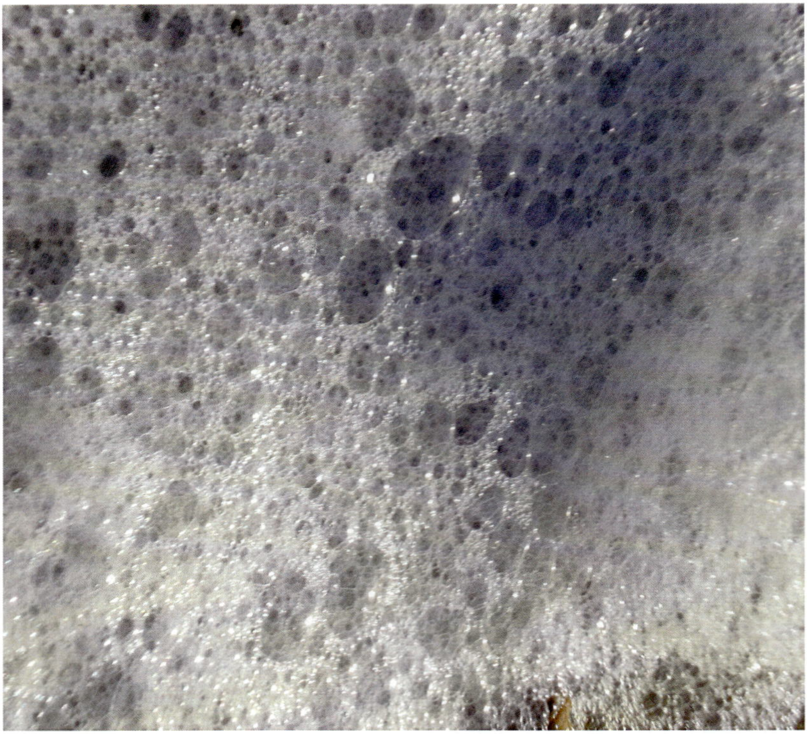

Possibilities

Prickly Bits

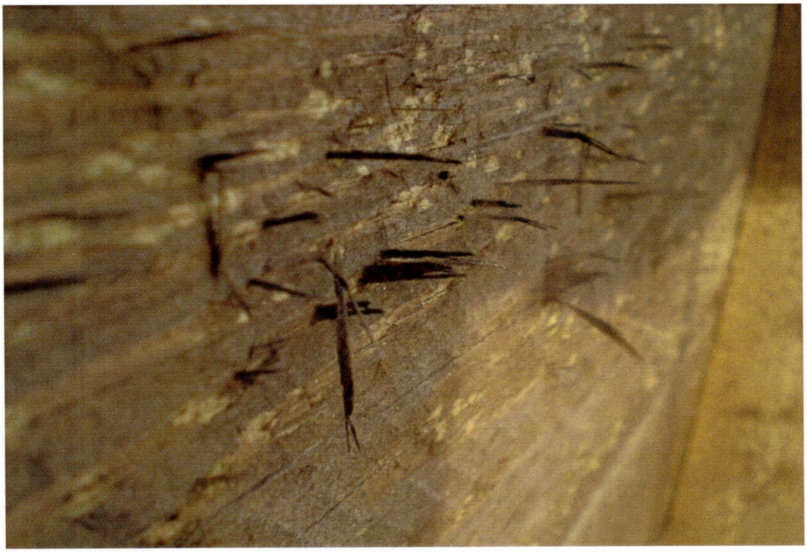

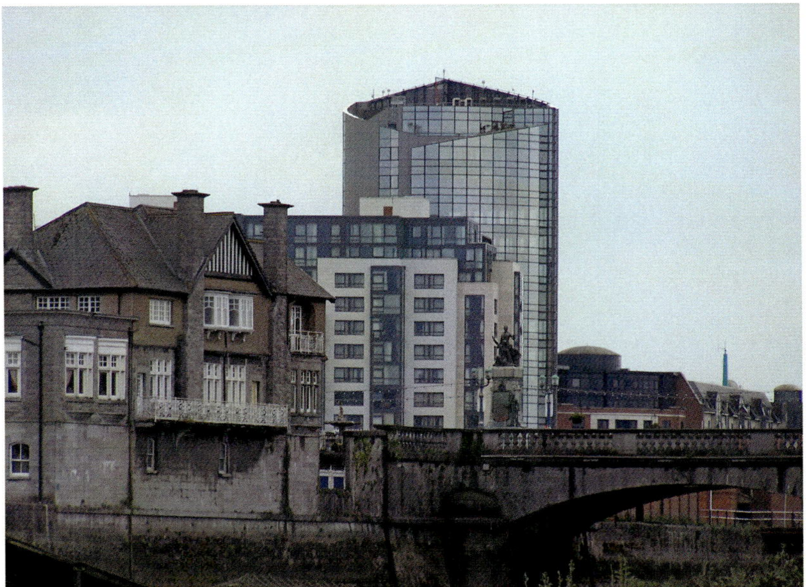

Progress

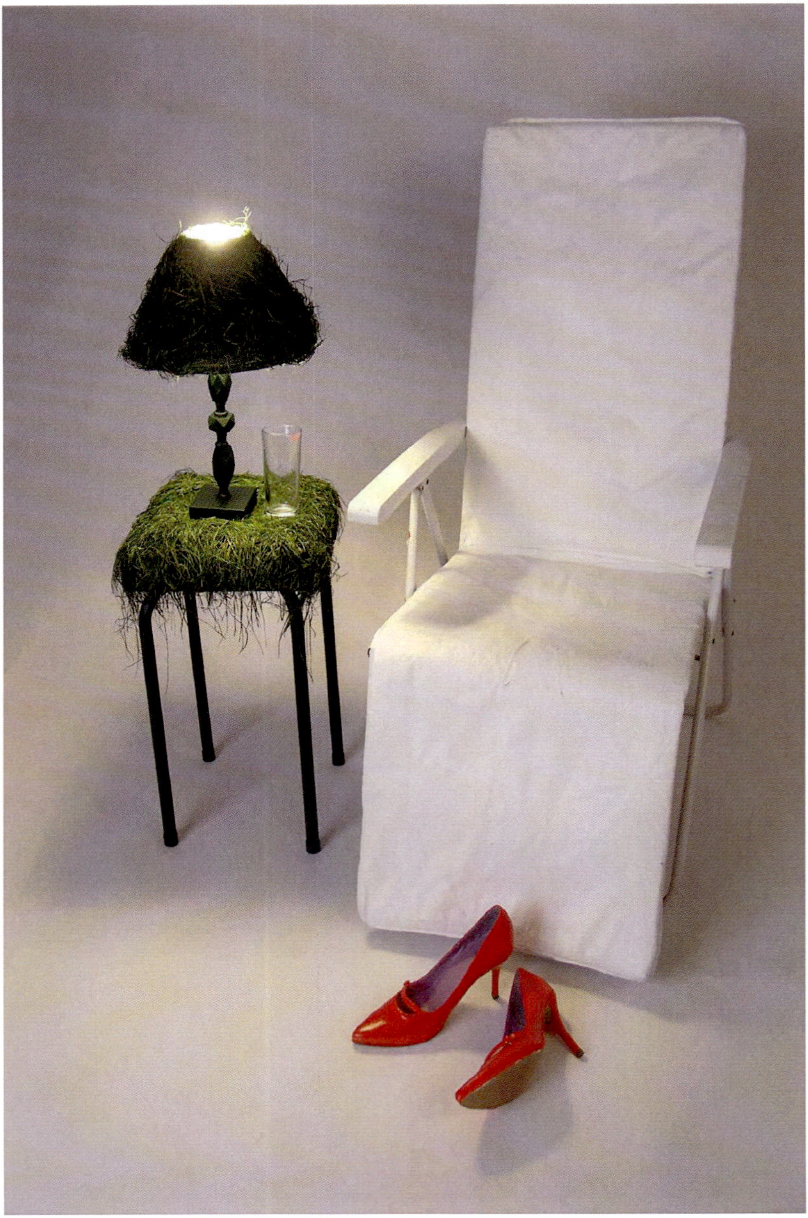

Quiet Moment

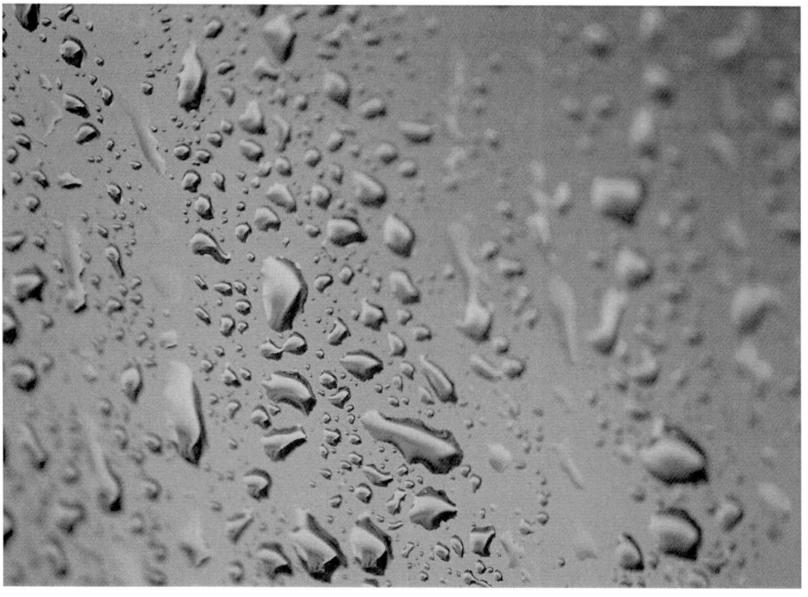

Raindrops Keep Falling

Reflection

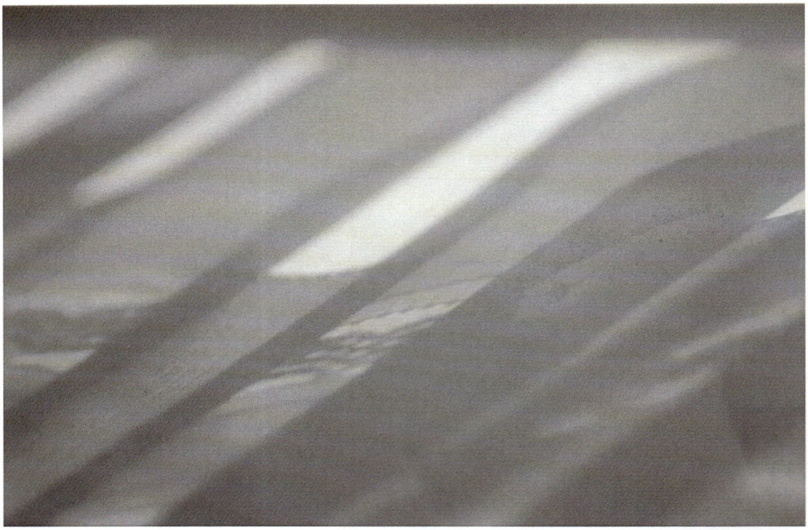

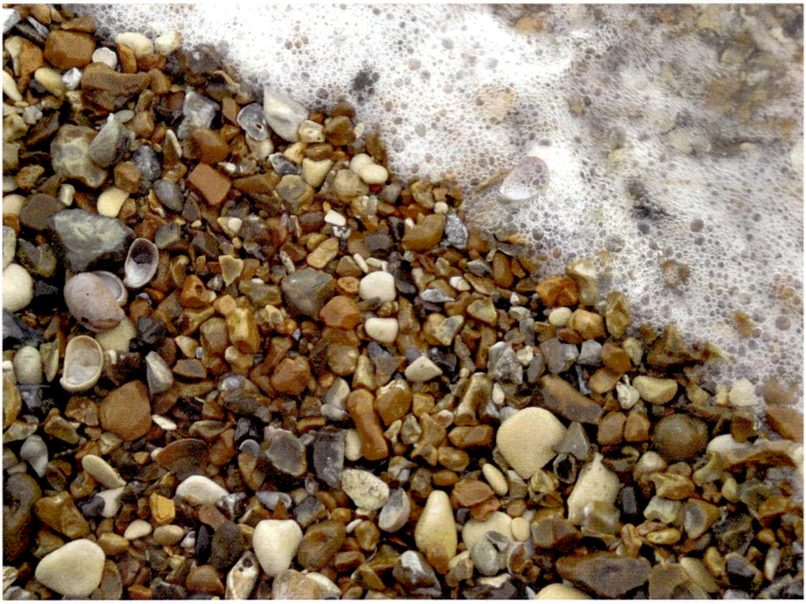

Refreshed

Rocks & Sea

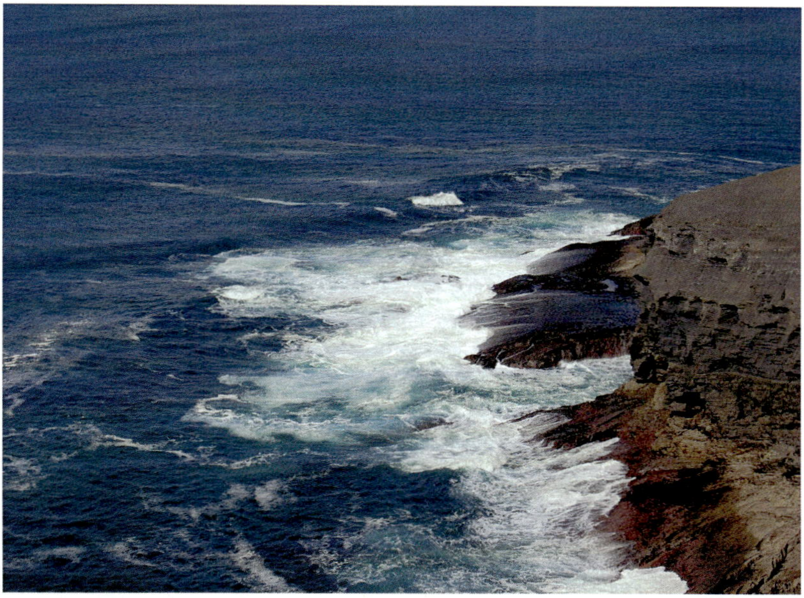

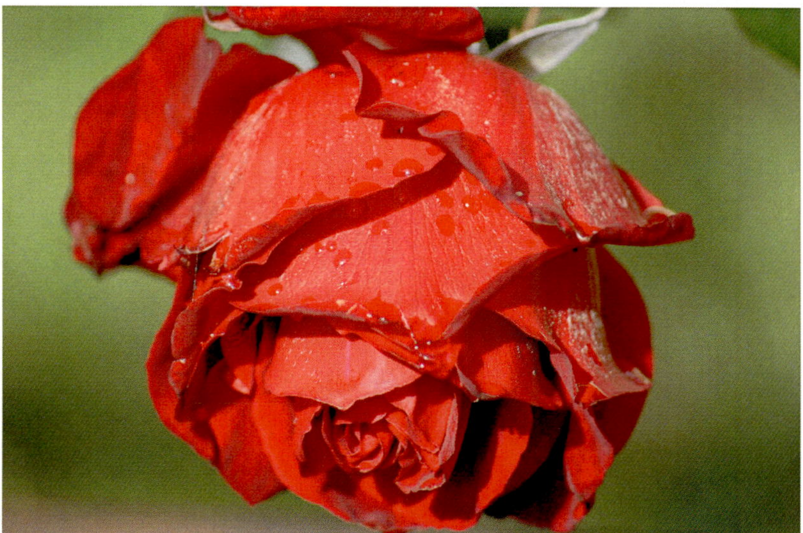

Rose

Rowing On The River

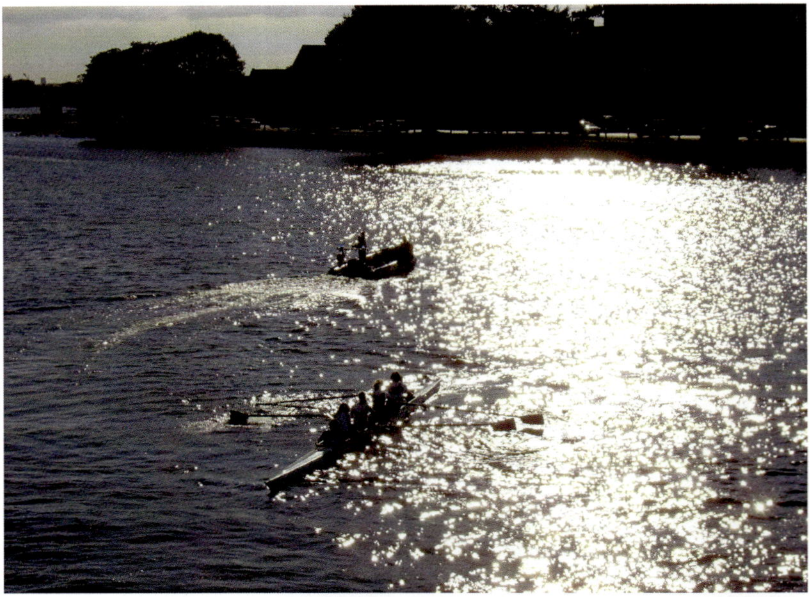

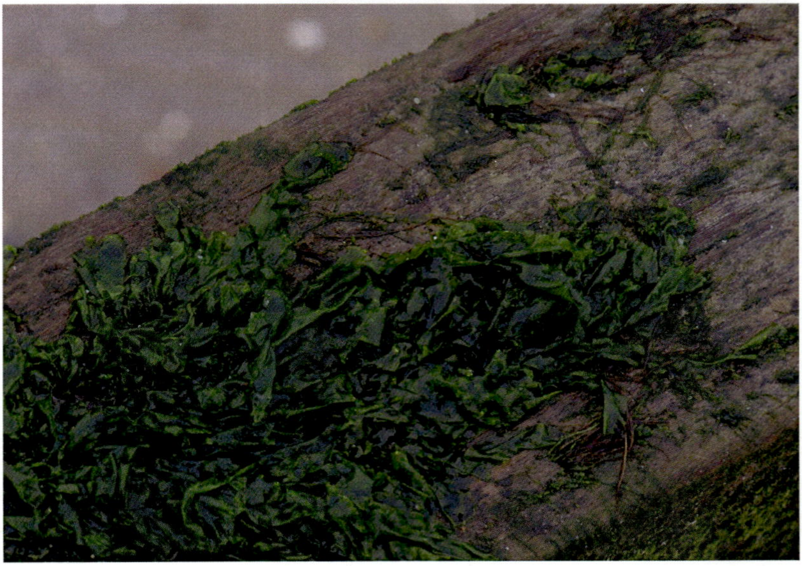

Seaweed

Shannon Sunset

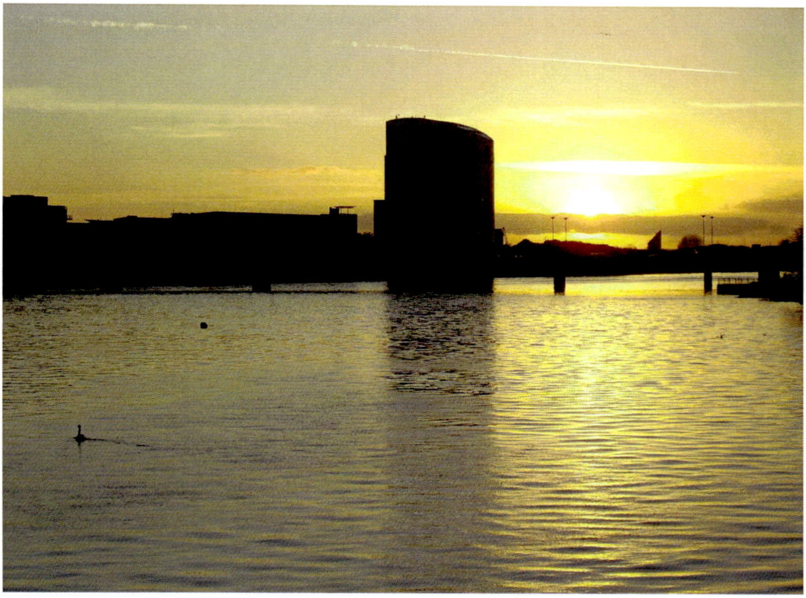

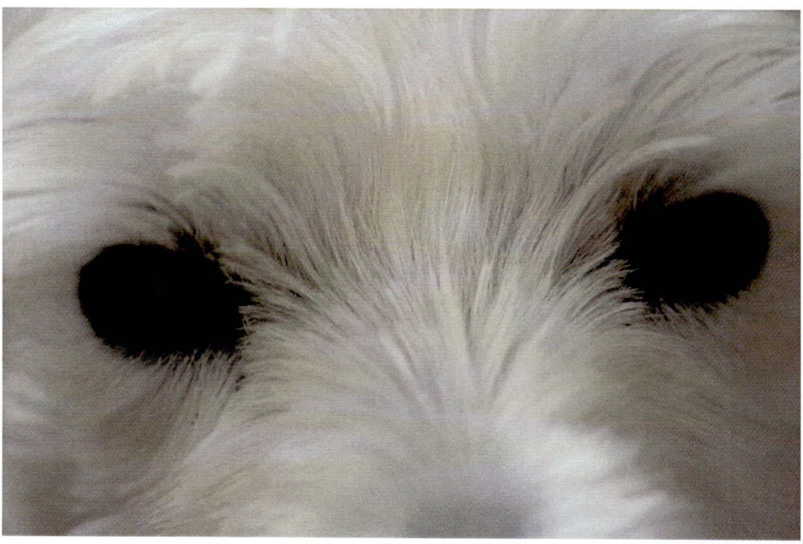

Shona

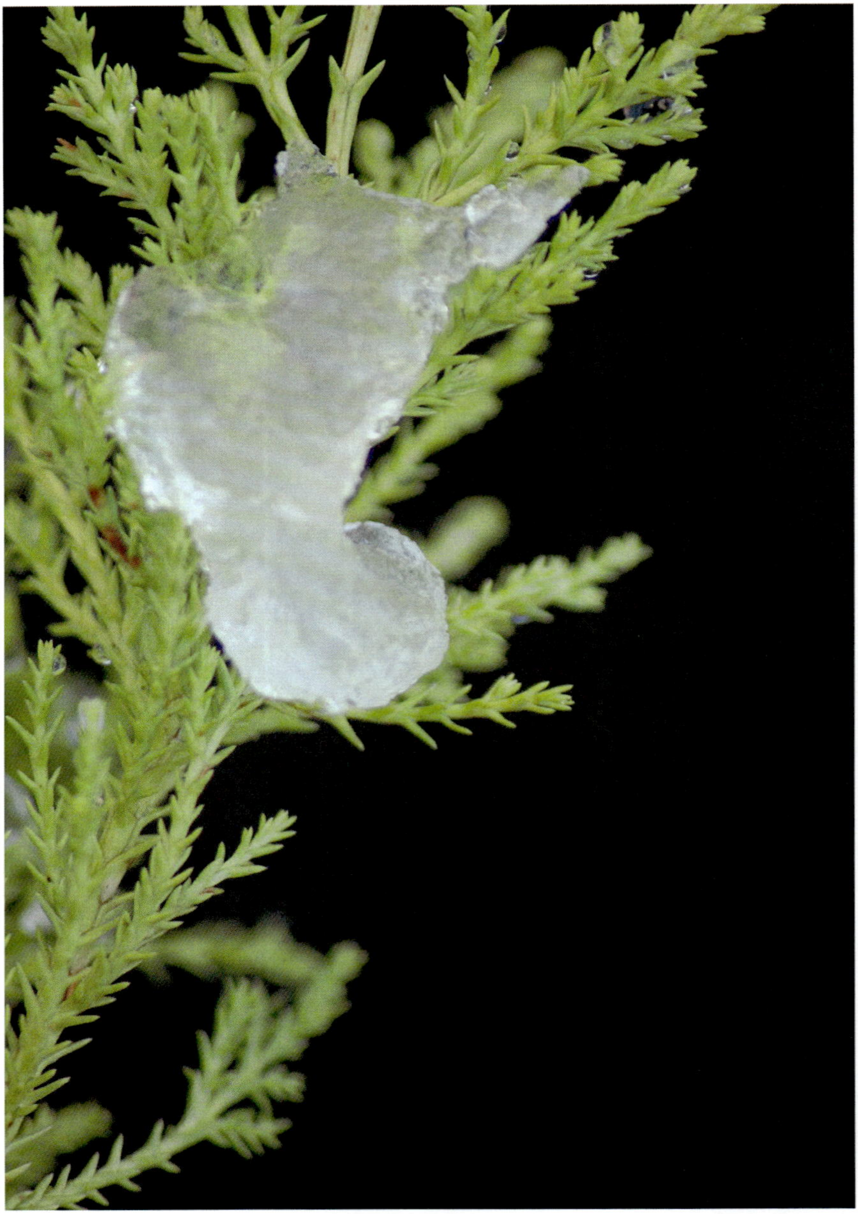

Slow Melt

Snow & Leaves

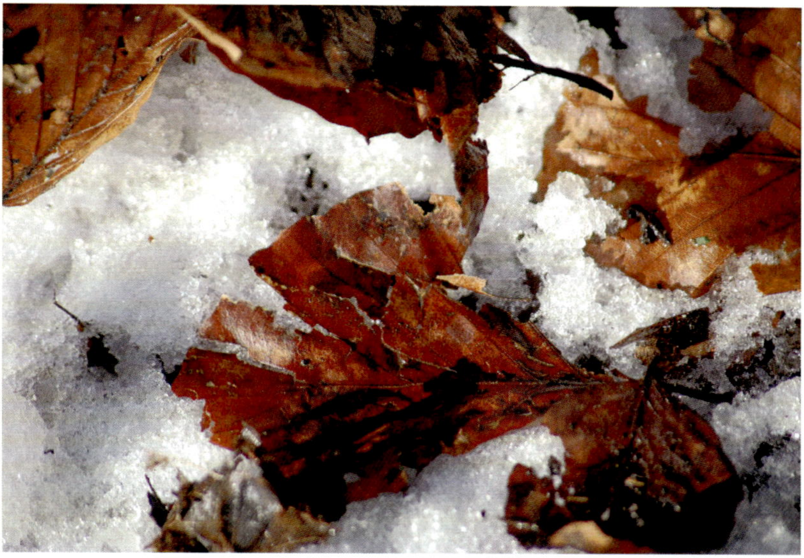

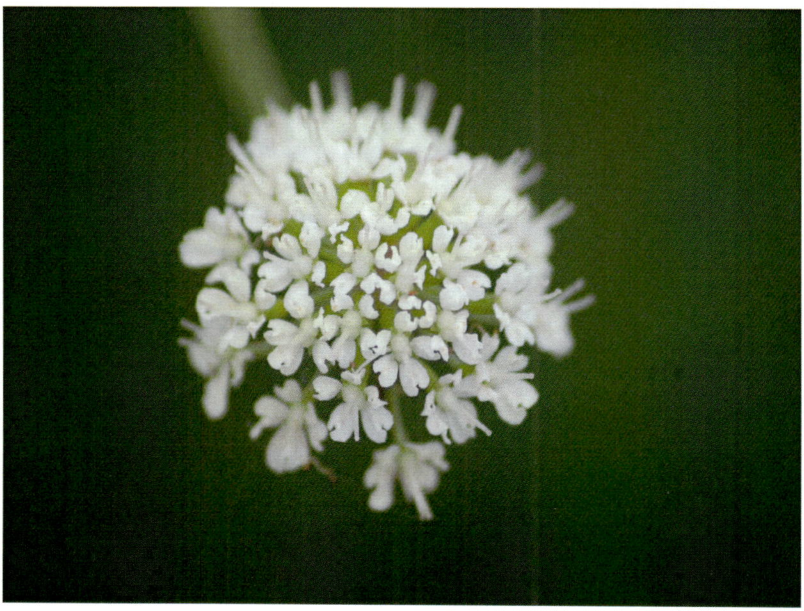

Solitary

Sour

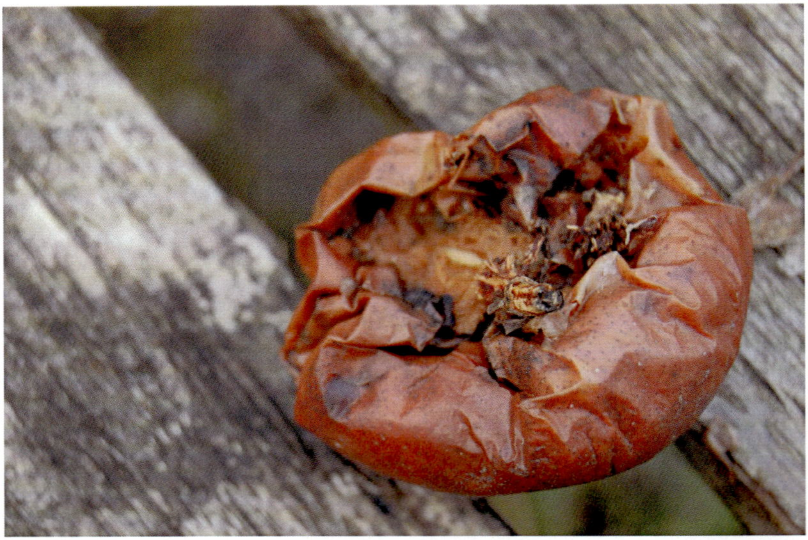

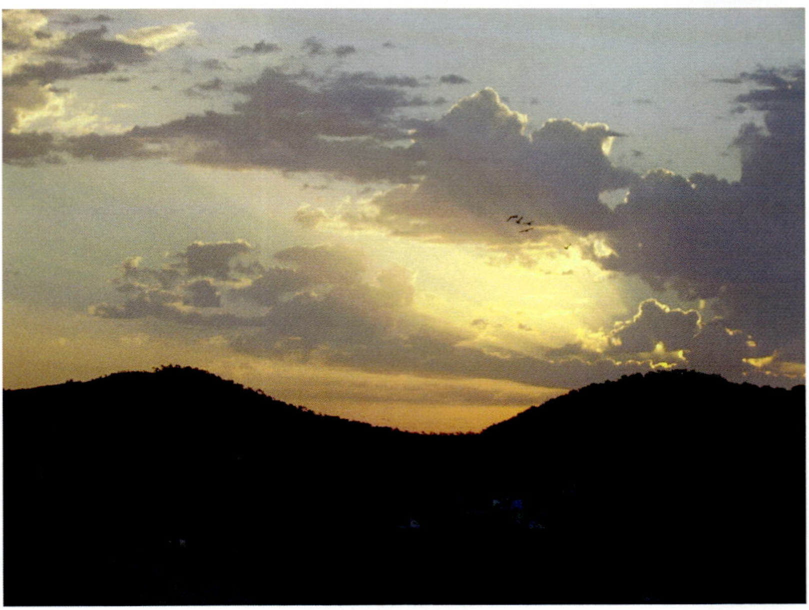

Spanish Dawn

Sparkling

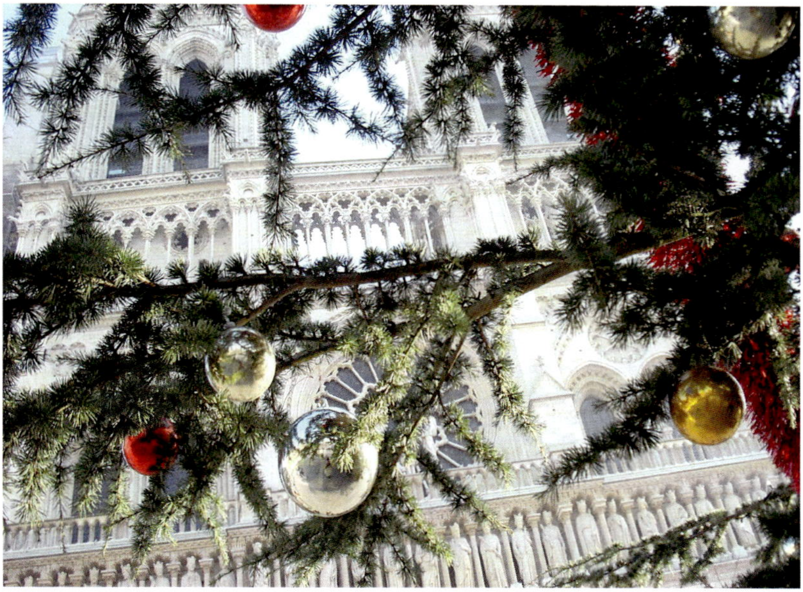

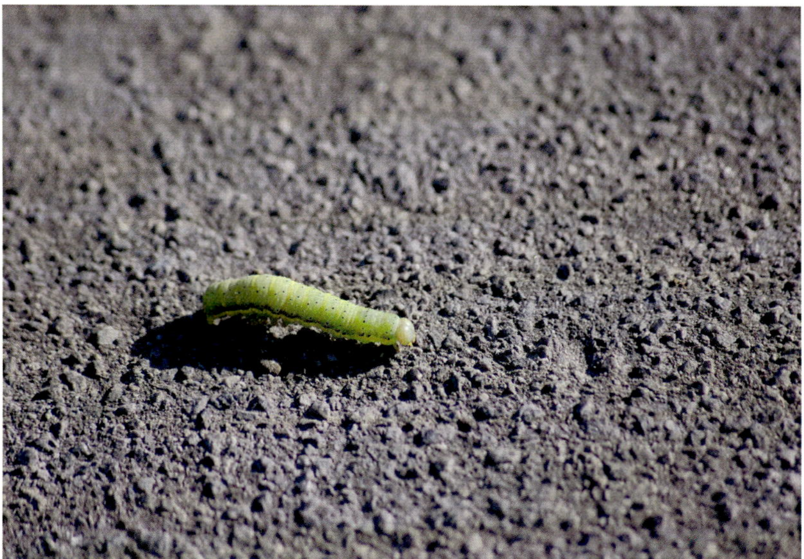

Speeding

Splash

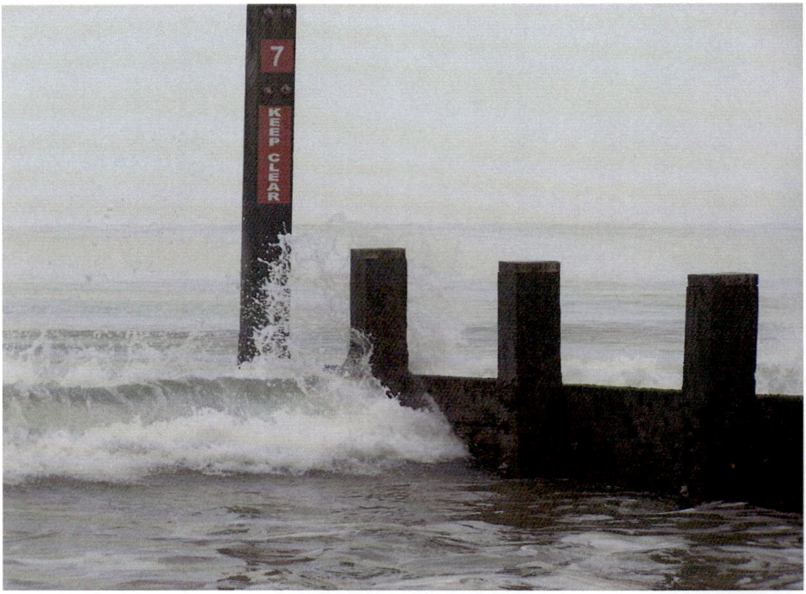

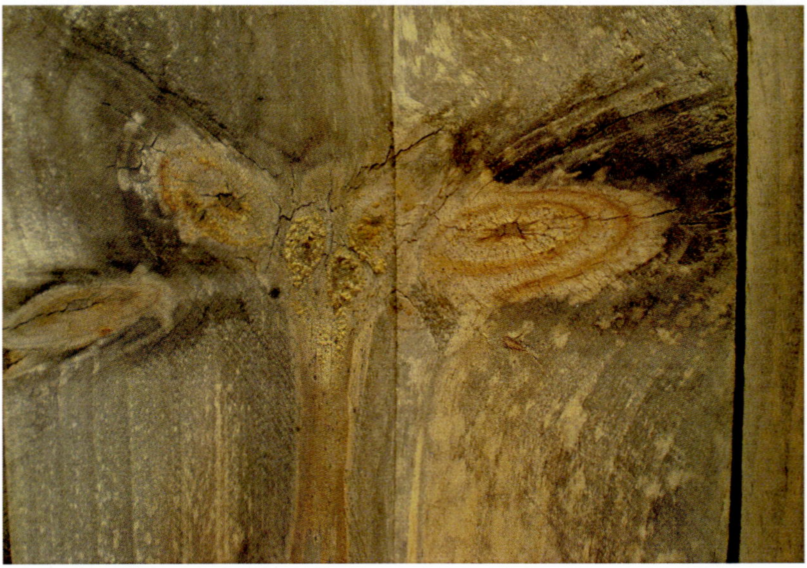

Stretched To The Limit

Submerged Rocks

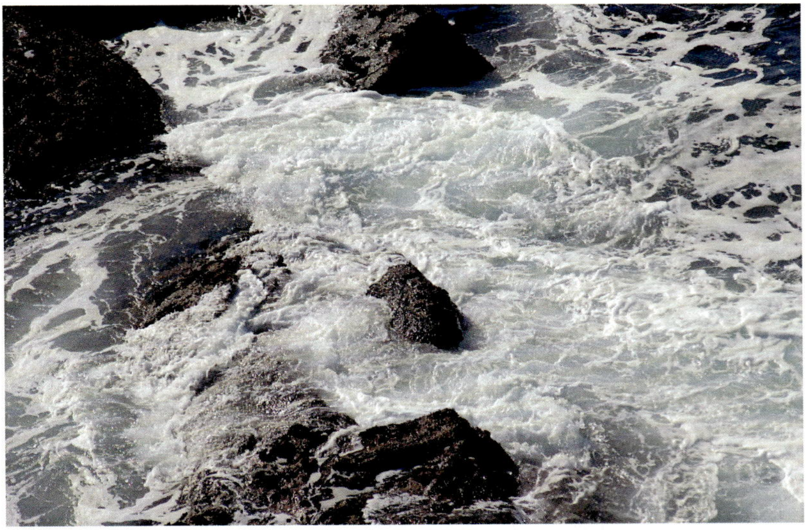

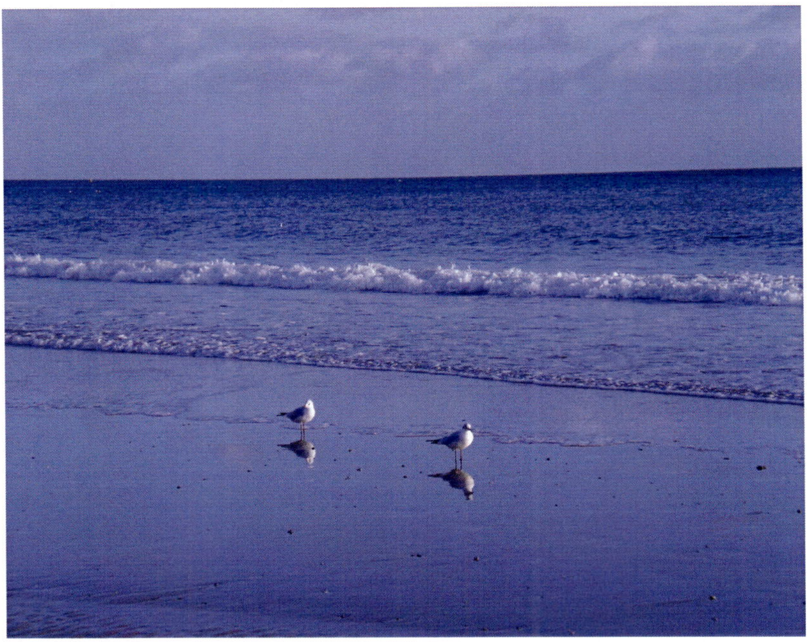

Taking A Stroll

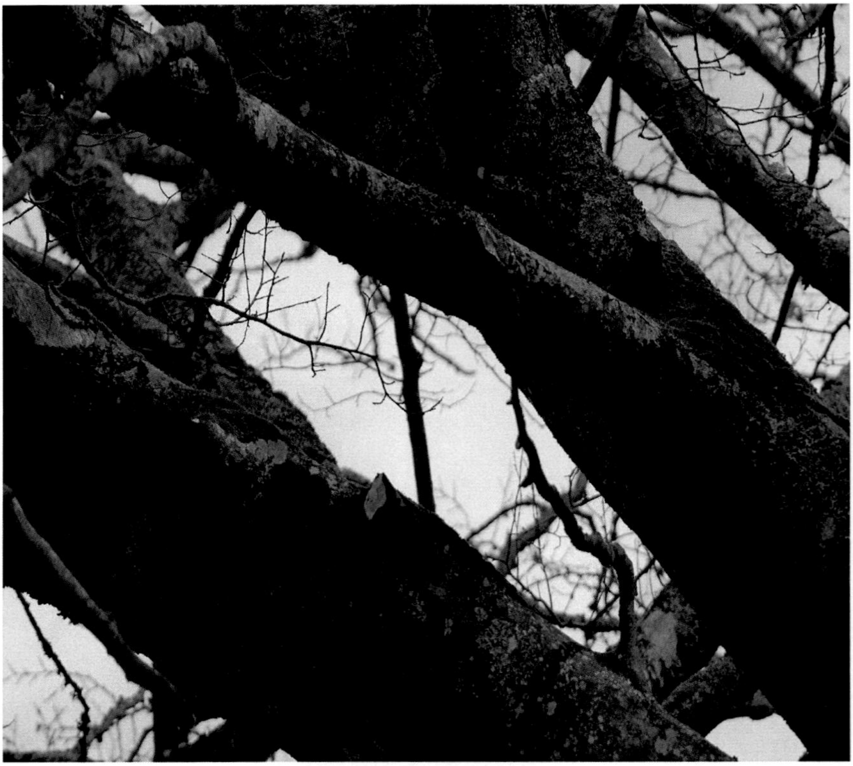

Tangled

Teddybed I

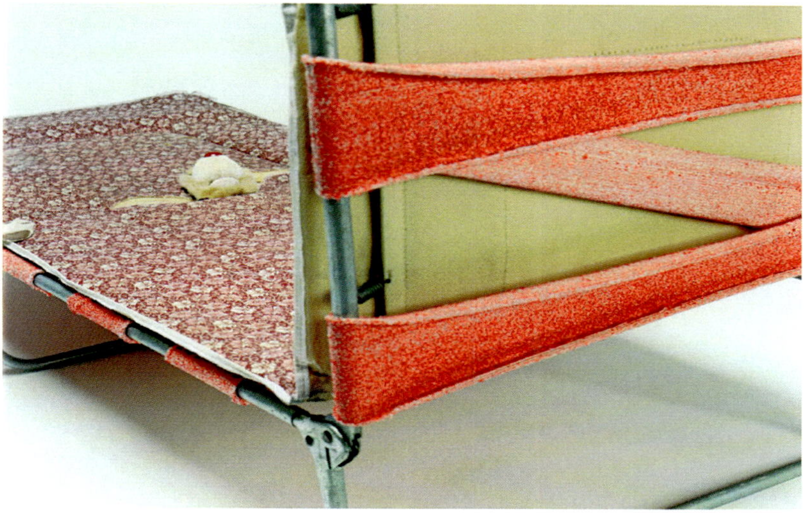

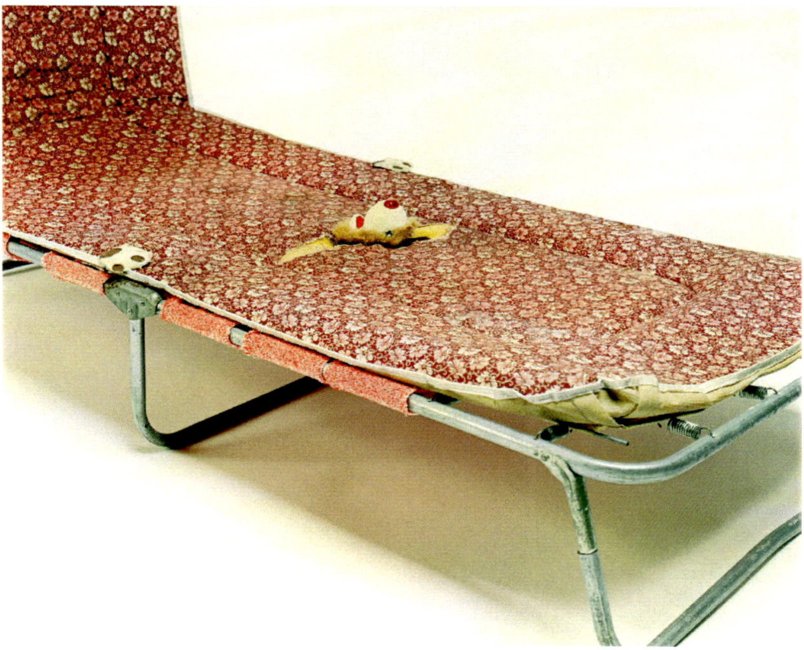

Teddybed II

The Pier

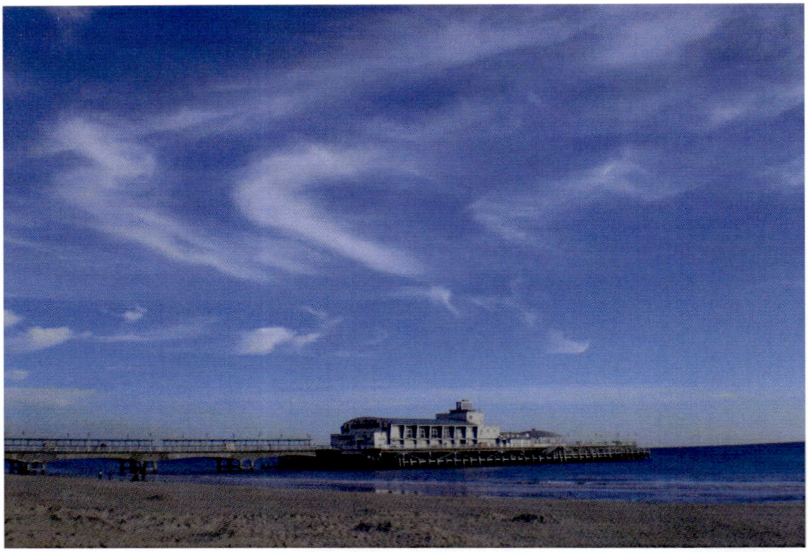

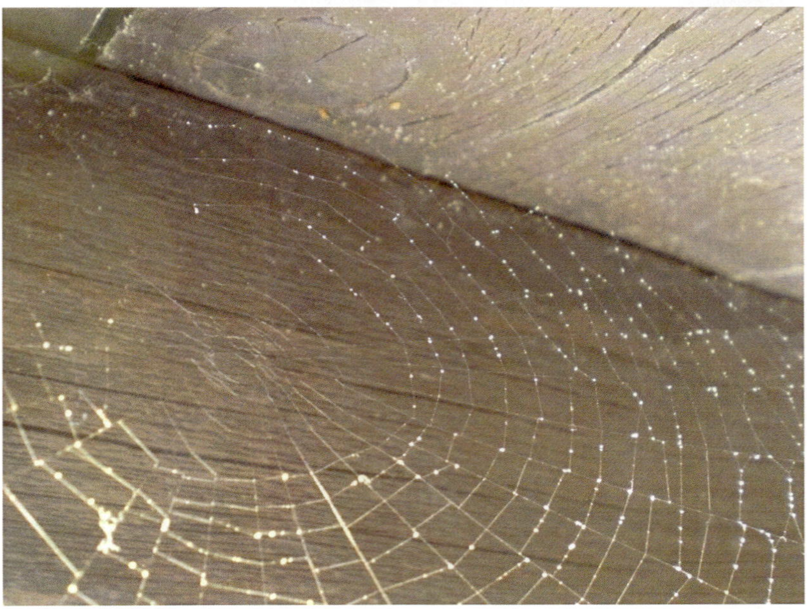

The Web

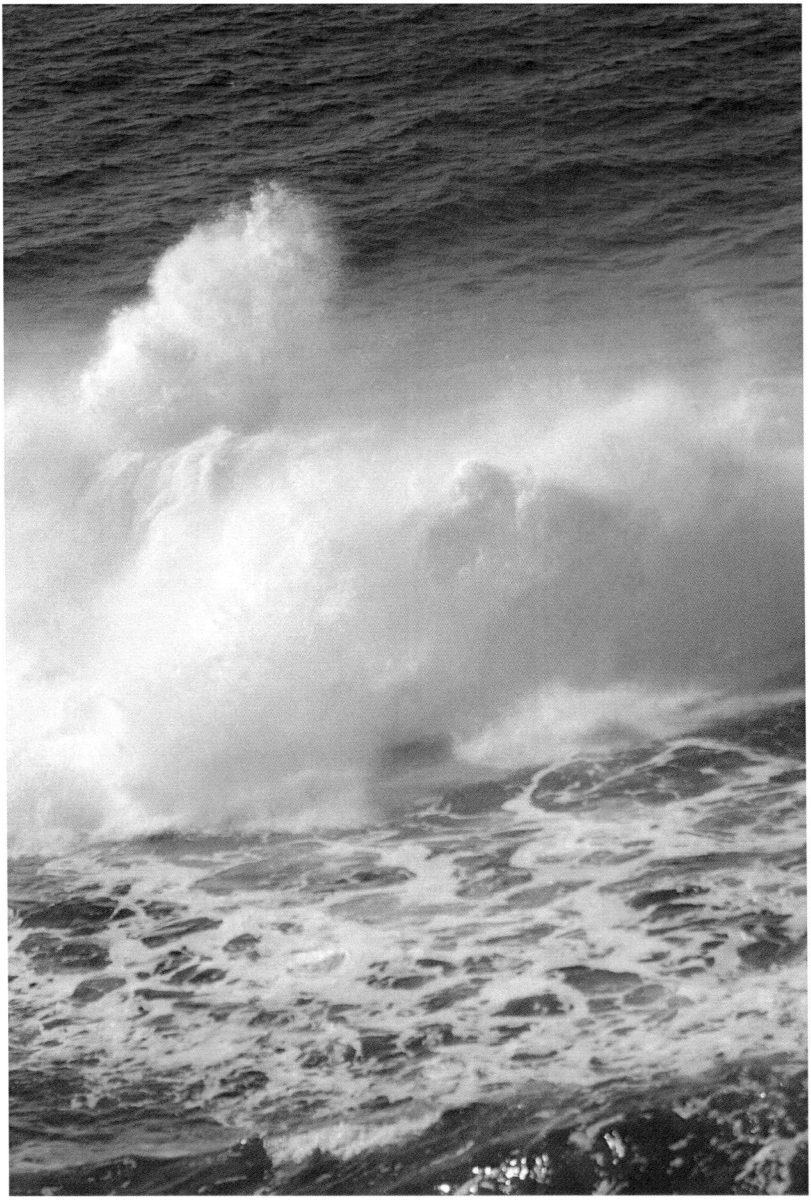

Turbulent

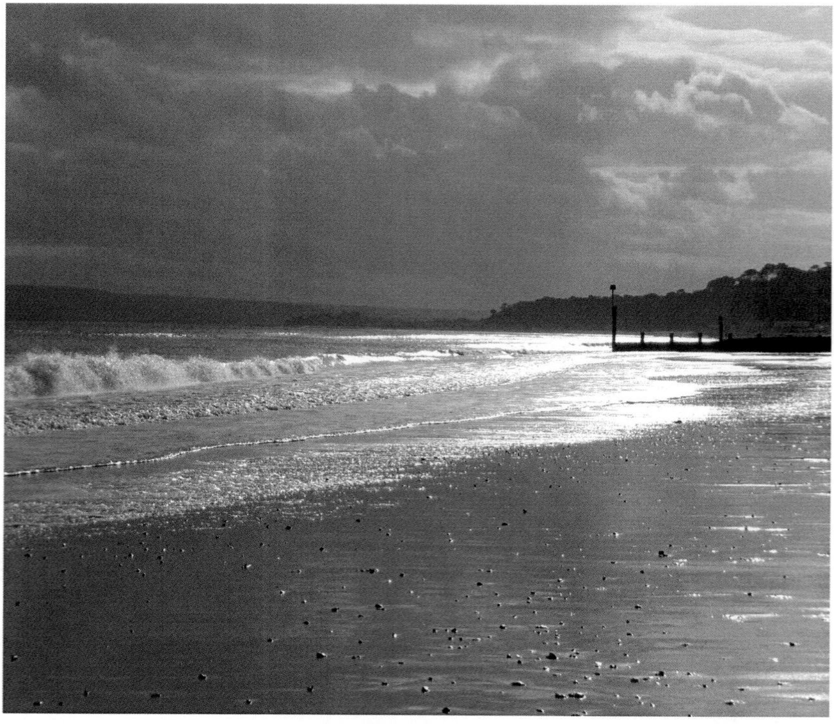

Twilight

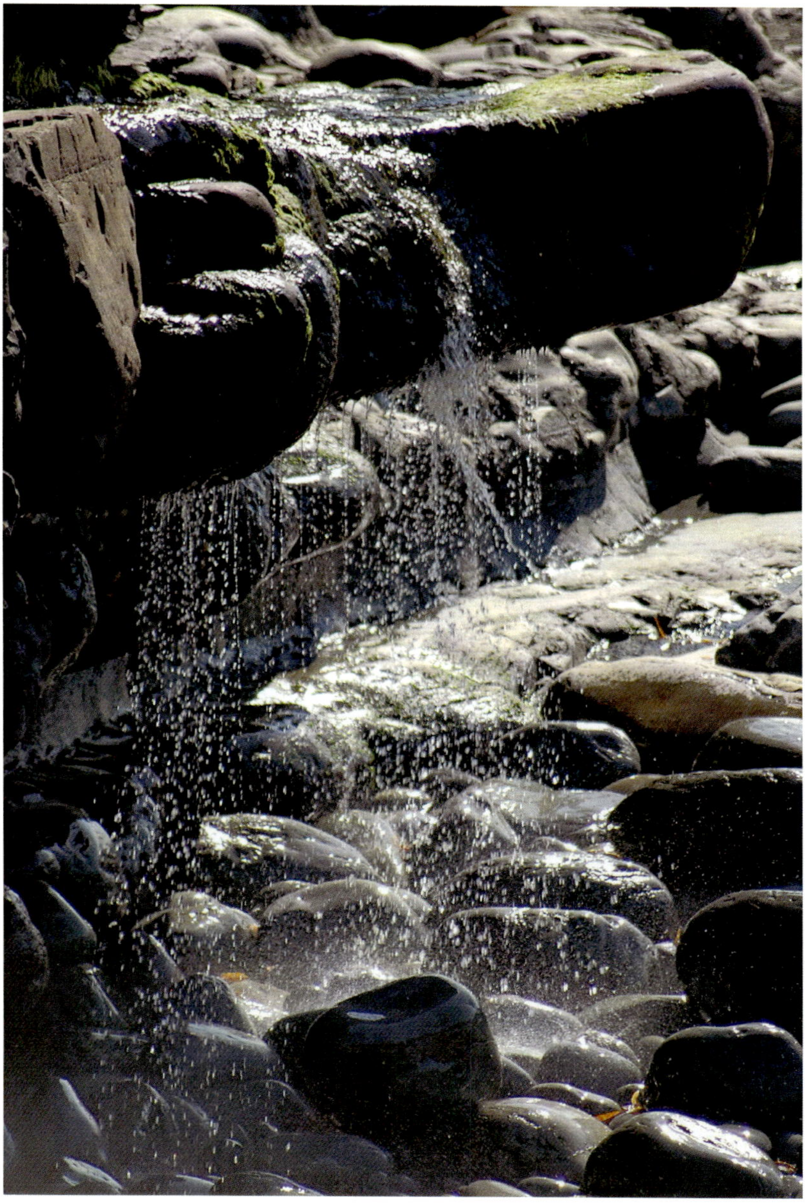

Unstoppable

Untitled (1)

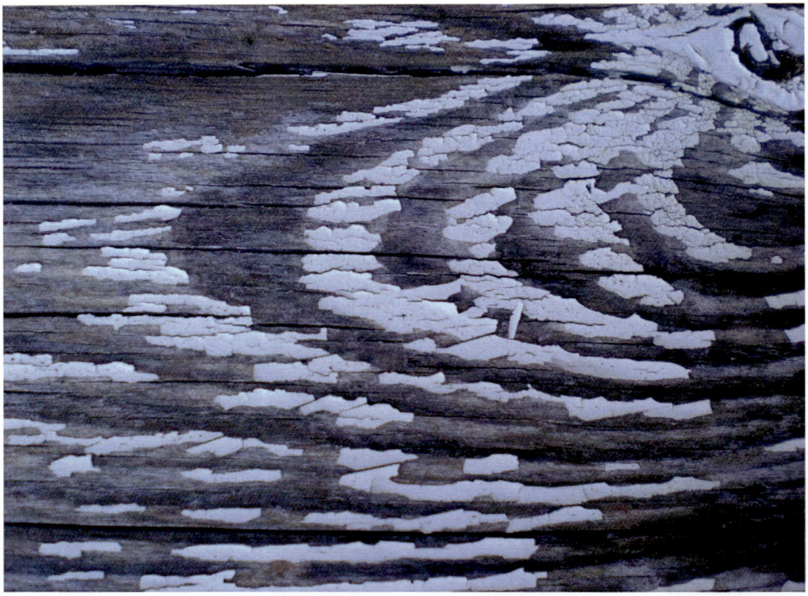

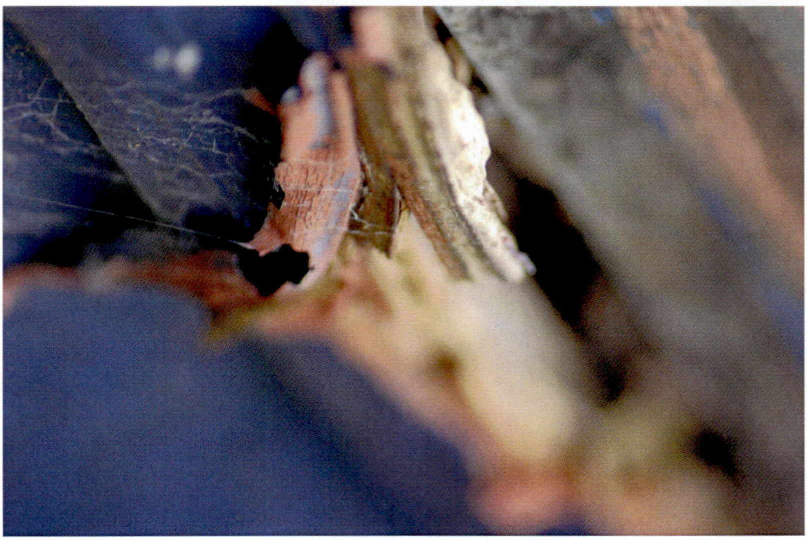

Untitled (2)

Urban Sunset

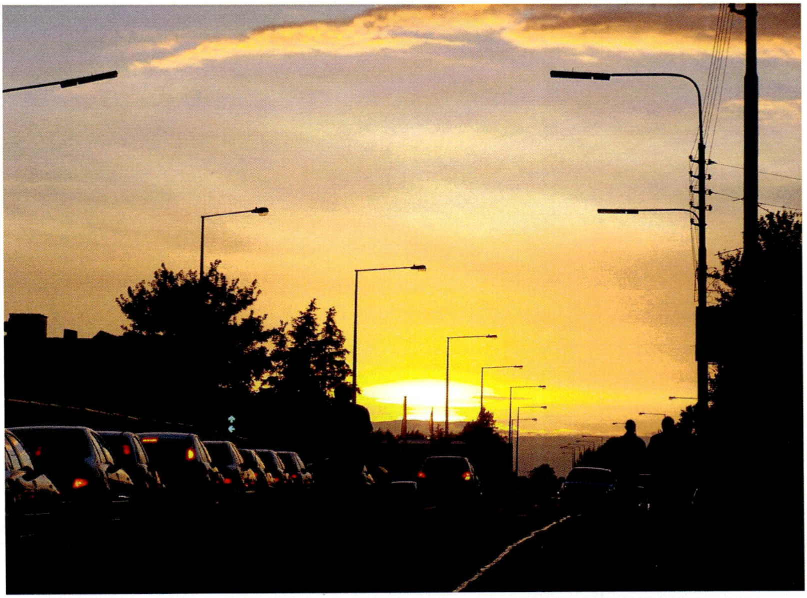

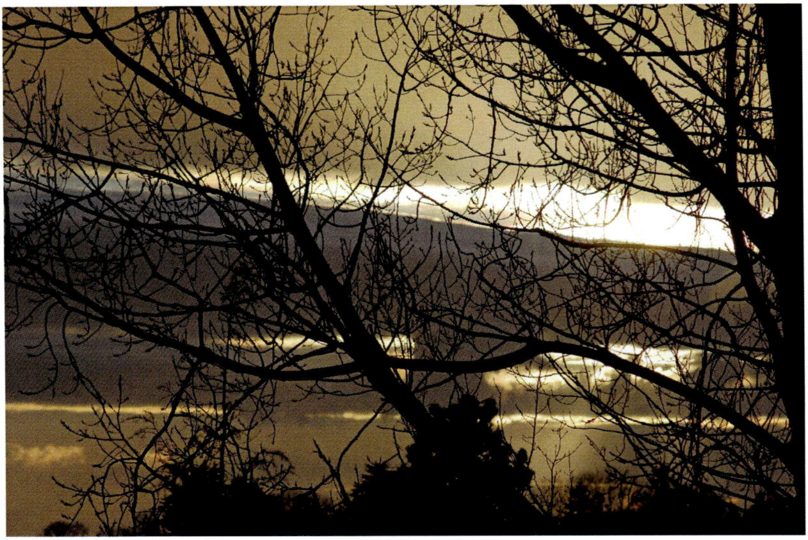

View From A Window

Waiting

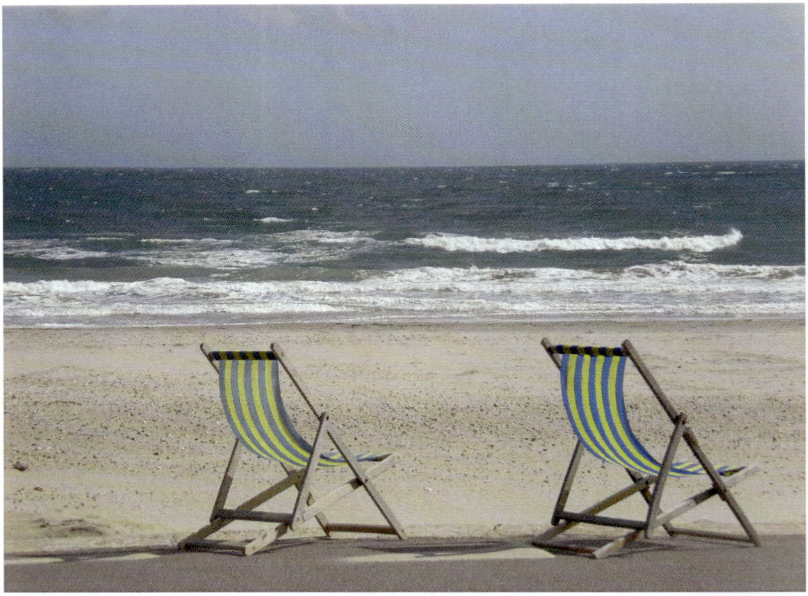

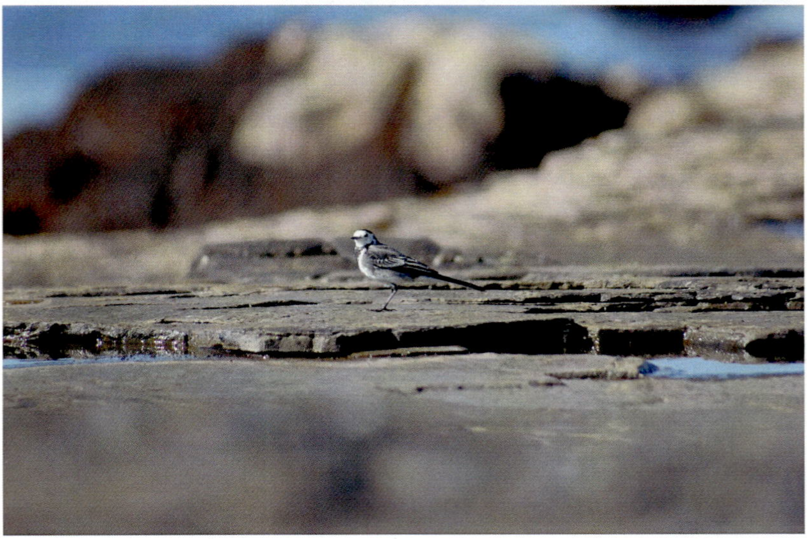

Watching

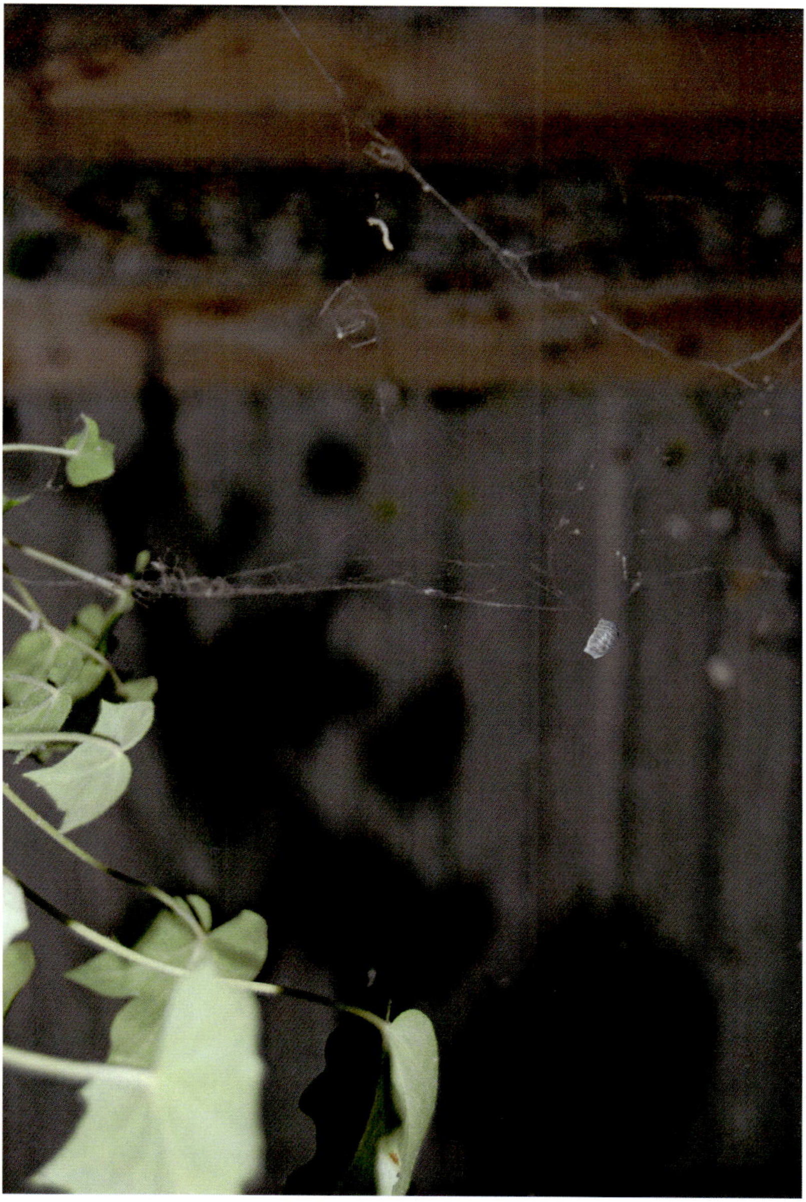

Web of Deceit

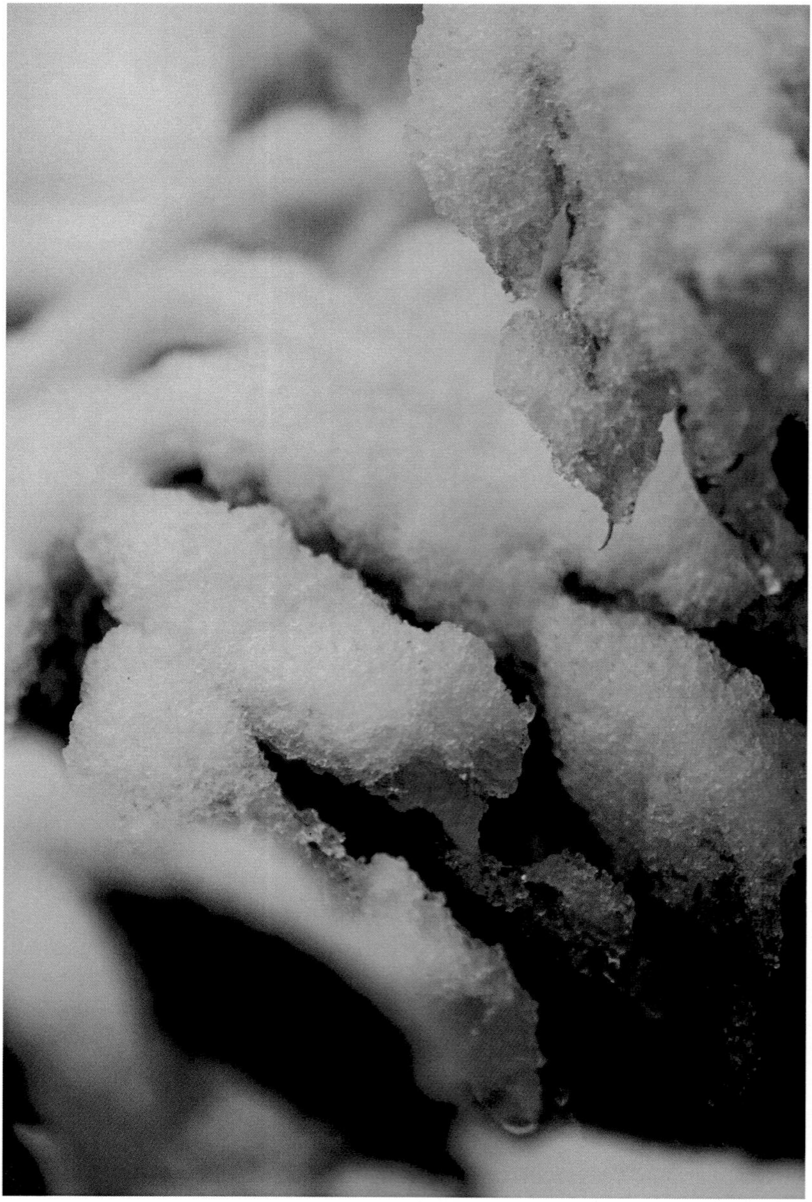

Weighted Down

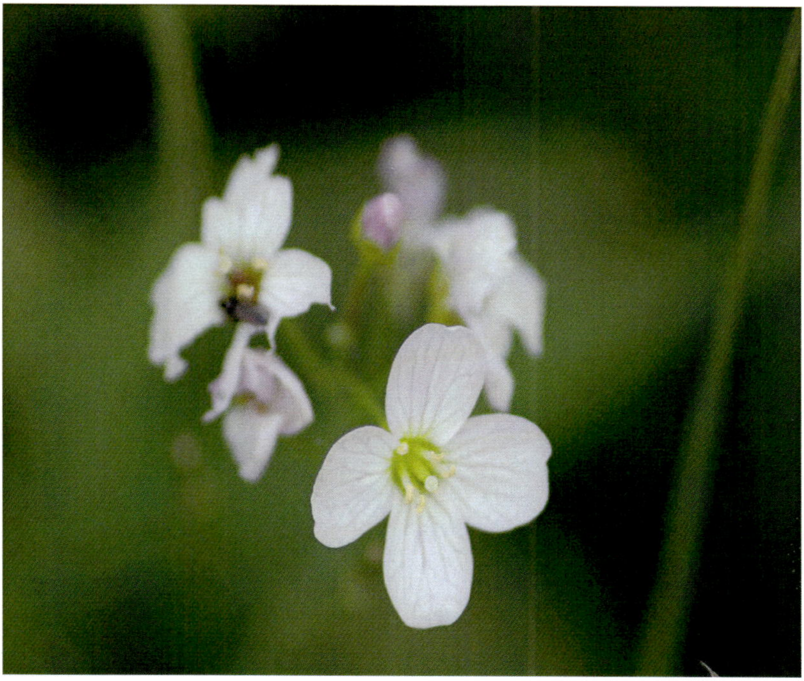

Wild Flower

Windswept

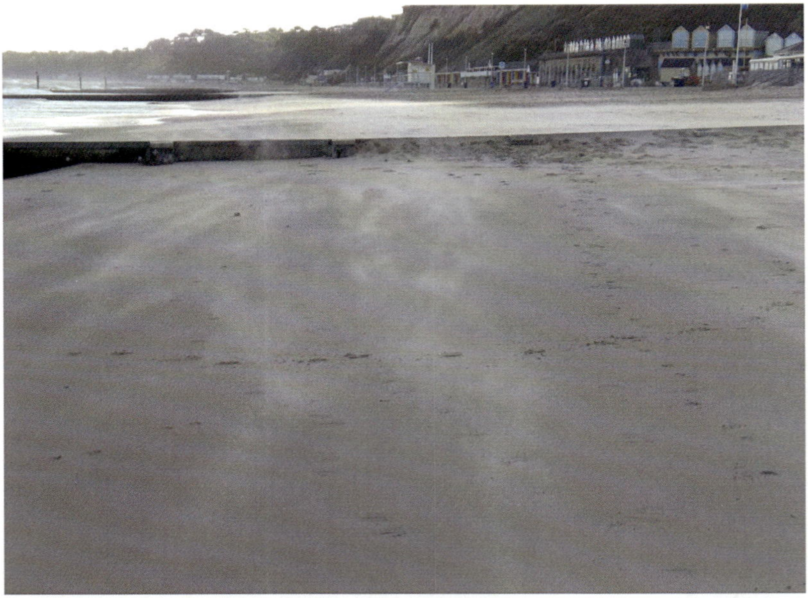

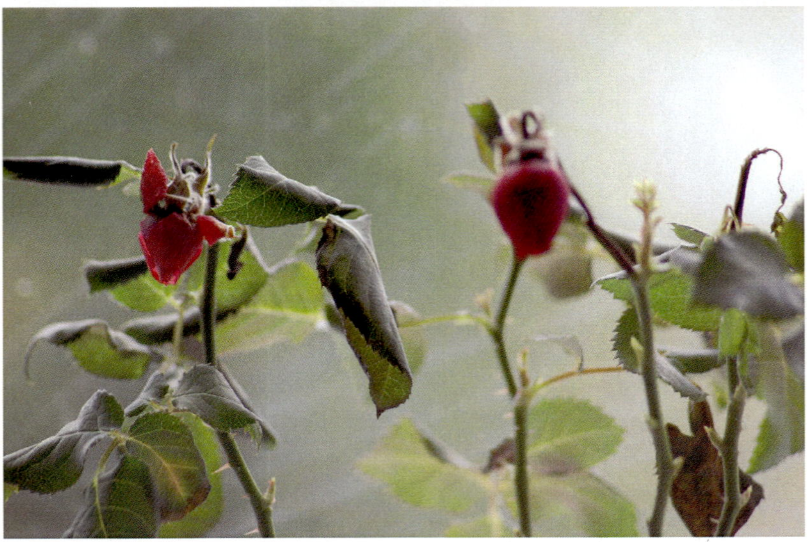

Withered Roses